Three Cases that Shook the Law

Ronald Bartle

≋ WATERSIDE PRESS

Three Cases that Shook the Law
Ronald Bartle

ISBN 978-1-909976-30-6 (Paperback)
ISBN 978-1-910979-06-8 (Epub ebook)
ISBN 978-1-910979-07-5 (Adobe ebook)

Copyright © 2016 This work is the copyright of Ronald Bartle. All intellectual property and associated rights are hereby asserted and reserved by him in full compliance with UK, European and international law. No part of this book may be copied, reproduced, stored in any retrieval system or transmitted in any form or by any means, or in any language, including in hard copy or via the internet, without the prior written permission of the publishers to whom all such rights have been assigned worldwide.

Cover design © 2016 Waterside Press. Pen icon made by Freepik from www.flaticon.com

Main UK distributor Gardners Books, 1 Whittle Drive, Eastbourne, East Sussex, BN23 6QH. Tel: +44 (0)1323 521777; sales@gardners.com; www.gardners.com

North American distribution Ingram Book Company, One Ingram Blvd, La Vergne, TN 37086, USA. Tel: (+1) 615 793 5000; inquiry@ingramcontent.com

Cataloguing-In-Publication Data A catalogue record for this book can be obtained from the British Library.

Printed by Lightning Source.

e-book *Three Cases that Shook the Law* is available as an ebook and also to subscribers of Myilibrary, Dawsonera, ebrary, and Ebscohost.

Published 2016 by
Waterside Press
Sherfield Gables
Sherfield-on-Loddon
Hook, Hampshire
United Kingdom RG27 0JG

Telephone +44(0)1256 882250
E-mail enquiries@watersidepress.co.uk
Online catalogue WatersidePress.co.uk

Table of Contents

About the author *v*
Acknowledgements *vi*
Dedication *vii*

Introduction 9

PART 1: EDITH JESSIE THOMPSON 19

1. **The Background Story** 21
   The Marriage of Percy and Edith *22*
   The Road to Murder *26*
   The Letters *30*
2. **The Murder of Percy Thompson** 35
3. **The Trial: The Scene is Set** 45
4. **The Indictment** 51
5. **The Opening Speech of the Solicitor-General** 61
6. **The Evidence for the Prosecution** 73
7. **The Evidence of Frederick Bywaters and Edith Thompson** 87
8. **The Closing Speeches of Counsel** 99
9. **The Summing-up** 105
10. **The Final Tragedy** 113

PART 2: WILLIAM JOYCE 115

11. **The Trial of William Joyce: Introduction** 117
12. **The Indictment** 127
13. **The Opening Speech for the Crown** 133
14. **Submission by the Defence on Counts One and Two** 137
15. **The Evidence for the Crown** 139

   Statement of offence *139*
   Particulars of offence *139*
16 **Crown and Defence Submission on Count Three**..................143
   Further Submission by the Prosecution *149*
17 **The Judge's Summing-up**..157
18 **The Appeal**...161
19 **Conclusion**...163

PART 3: TIMOTHY EVANS 165

20 **Introduction: The Trial of Timothy Evans**...............................167
21 **The Opening Submissions**...183
   The Judge's Ruling *183*
22 **The Prosecution Case**...189
23 **The Defence Case**..223
24 **Speeches and Summing up**...229
25 **The Aftermath**..233
   The Inquiries *234*

Index *236*

About the author

Ronald Bartle was Deputy Chief Stipendiary Magistrate (now District Judge) for Inner London. His books include *The Telephone Murder: The Mysterious Death of Julia Wallace* (2012); *The Police Witness: A Guide to Presenting Evidence in Court* (1984 onwards) and *Bow Street Beak* (Foreword Lord Hurd of Westwell) (2000).

Acknowledgements

The author wishes to acknowledge the following sources:
Trial of Bywaters and Thompson, Notable British Trials, 1923/1951.
Great Cases of Sir Henry Curtis Bennett, Edward Grice, 1937.
The Innocence of Edith Thompson, Lewis Broad, 1952.
A Book of Trials, Sir Travers Humphreys, 1953.
United in Crime, H Montgomery Hyde, 1955.
Great True Crime Stories — Women, Pamela Search, 1957.
Verdict in Dispute, Edgar Lustgarten, 2010 (reprint).
Trial of William Joyce, Notable British Trials, 1946.
The Meaning of Treason, Rebecca West, 1982.
Trials of Christie and Evans, Notable British Trials, 1957.
10 Rillington Place, Ludovic Kennedy, 1961.

To my wife Molly

With grateful thanks for all
her enthusiastic support
and encouragement.

Three Cases that Shook the Law

Introduction

This book is concerned with three serious miscarriages of justice: the cases involved are those of Edith Jessie Thompson in 1922, William Joyce in 1945 and Timothy Evans in 1950.

It should be said at the outset that it is not the contention of this author that any of the defendants was proved to be innocent. If the burden of proof lay upon the defence it is probable that none of the three would have been able to discharge it in a court of law. Yet nothing is clearer in British courts than that the burden of proof rests with the prosecution and remains as such throughout the case. It never shifts to the defence. The judge will remind the jury of this basic and indeed vital rule of our jurisprudence. Nevertheless a situation may develop where this canon of the criminal law may become obscured.

A jury consists of 12 men and women with no expertise either in the law or the weighing of evidence but who are nevertheless entrusted, by the application of common sense, with the question of guilt or innocence. Almost invariably they discharge their onerous duty honestly and well. But jury men and women are human and are subject to human imperfection.

Although they will be reminded by the judge in his or her summing-up that they must not make up their minds until after full discussion of the case in their room it is sometimes inevitable that their view of the witnesses and their veracity is formed during the conduct of the trial. This is particularly the case where the defendant chooses to give evidence on his or her own behalf. If a defendant makes a very bad impression on the members of the jury, or on a number of them, the defence may be placed in the position of having to endeavour to rehabilitate their client. The atmosphere of the trial changes to the advantage of the prosecution.

The judge cannot be constantly reminding the jury members of their duty not to make hasty decisions. He cannot during the hearing intervene to emphasise to them that the defendant remains innocent until proved guilty to their entire satisfaction. The burden of proof remains in law upon the prosecution, but the struggling defender may well feel that it has now shifted to him to prove his client is innocent.

It is a principle of evidence in criminal trials that the jury may not only draw their conclusions from the facts which they hear, but they may draw from one fact a reasonable inference that another fact is also true. Again, the judge will assist them, but he cannot give a definition which fits the particular circumstance of each case. When is an inference reasonable? When is it not? And when is it merely a presumption—which may be erroneous. Jury trial is an admirable system of justice, but juries are not always right.

Judges also are not above the pitfalls of their profession. The fundamental quality of the good judge is impartiality and absence of bias. But there are times when this high ideal can amount almost to a counsel of perfection. In English courts of law, unlike American, the function of the judge is to direct the jury on the law and to sum up the facts so far as is necessary to help them to reach the correct verdict. It is in regard to the second of these duties that the problem arises.

A judge would be extraordinarily infallible if he never entertained his own private view of the case before him. He or she is entitled in summing-up to give effect to what he or she sees as a correct interpretation of the facts, and do what he or she regards as correct. But this can be a precarious exercise.

To criticise the way in which one side or the other has presented its case can easily look like bias. That is why some judges become known at the Bar as "prosecution-minded". An extreme example of the former applies to a London judge some years ago. During the course of an interview regarding his judicial office, he said that he saw his function as "ensuring that nobody pulled the wool over the eyes of the jury". That meant in practice that in almost every case he tried he used his office for the purpose of convicting the accused person.

A further consideration is the attitude of the persons on the jury to the judge. This is important because the jury, while obliged to follow the direction of the judge on the law, does not, if it so chooses, have to adopt his recommendations on the facts. That attitude of the laity towards the judiciary has undoubtedly changed over the years. The aura of authority and superior wisdom enjoyed by what is called "the ruling class" or "the establishment" years ago no longer applies. Judges, Cabinet Ministers, bishops and the like were, up to a point, assumed to possess superior wisdom otherwise they would not occupy the positions that they did. The judge has expressed his or her view and we should give great weight to what he or she has said. This view certainly appertained in the early years of the last century. I shall in due course expand in this factor in the chapter regarding the Thompson-Bywaters trial in 1922.

No longer are judges accorded the deference which they once were. They, like juries, are seen as humanly fallible. In his book *The Judges and the Judged* (1926, p.2) Charles Kingston writes:

> "The question of erroneous verdicts will continue to the end of time. Someone may invent an infallible jury but by then the world will have ceased to be populated by human beings, and until then justice will have its ups and downs. Judges will always have their fads and counsel will not disdain trickery in fighting a desperate battle, while juries, if they wish, will exercise the right of the free born to display prejudice and partiality."

Finally a word about counsel. No profession has been more misunderstood than that of a barrister. Socially the position has always had a certain cachet. Yet in the eyes of many there is a tendency to look askance at the work of defending in the criminal court. The usual and somewhat time worn question is: "How can you defend someone whom you know to be guilty?" The question itself is based on a misunderstanding. It presumes that judge, counsel and perhaps the members of the jury have somehow acquired instinctive knowledge regarding the guilt or innocence of the defendant even before the trial, which after all is held to decide that very issue. A criminal trial is not held in order to give effect to any instinctive sense in the persons involved as to the guilt or otherwise of the accused. It takes place in order to provide the answer to the issue whether the individual who starts with the presumption of innocence has been proved on the evidence in fact to be guilty as charged.

A second consideration is that in a criminal trial of any significance the Crown is usually represented by counsel of some ability and experience. If the defendant did not enjoy the right of similar representation the trial would be hopelessly one-sided.

The early years of this century are considered to have been the "Golden Age of the English Bar". Edward Marshall Hall, Henry Curtis-Bennett, Norman Birkett and Patrick Hastings were household names. Yet the style of each was different. A cynic once said that a criminal trial was a test to see which side had the better barrister. This assessment is, happily, for humour. But it contains a slight element of truth. The ability of counsel can influence the result of the case. For instance, Marshall Hall is said to have believed that he could have won an acquittal for Edith Thompson. This is of course speculative, but it may be that his bold, passionate manner might have swayed the jury in his client's favour and that his boldness in standing-up to judges may have been more effective than Sir Henry Curtis-Bennett's more deferential manner towards Mr Justice Shearman.

We shall see how influential, in the three trials which are the subject of this work, is the behaviour of judge, counsel and jurors.

No trilogy of cases could be more disparate, while the reasons why their conclusions constitute a miscarriage of justice could not be more different. These matters, will of course, be explored much more fully in the forthcoming pages of this work. But let us, briefly in this introduction, examine the bare facts of each one and the causes why each has, over subsequent years, been considered by many lawyers to be so unsatisfactory and well below the traditionally high standards of British justice.

The conviction of Edith Thompson was against the weight of the evidence; that of William Joyce involved an unjustifiable extension of the law; and the verdict of guilty on Timothy Evans, later held to be "unsafe", may well have resulted in an innocent man being executed.

These matters will be explored in far greater detail in the following pages of this book. At this point I deal with them briefly for introductory purposes.

The King against Thompson and Bywaters is a story of romance turned to murder, or perhaps to put it more colloquially an instance of the eternal triangle. The events leading up to the tragedy can be stated fairly simply. Edith Thompson was an intelligent and attractive young woman who was in steady employment. At the time of her marriage to Percy Thompson she was 22 and he some three years older but relatively staid. Such a difference is not necessarily any bar to happiness in a marriage, but it is clear from what one learns about their matrimonial history, that Edith and Percy were not well matched. The debate concerning the ingredients which go into the making of a happy marriage is endless and will probably never be concluded.

In her evidence in court Edith said that the first two years were reasonably happy. After that there were frequent differences and quarrels. The fact that there were no children of their union and that each had their own separate employment tended to increase the division between them. Into their lives came Frederick Bywaters.

In contrast to Percy, Bywaters was eight years younger and attractive, with a good record. He worked as a ship's clerk which meant he was away at sea for much of the time. Thompson, perhaps somewhat naïvely encouraged the friendship of his wife and himself with Frederick, but the amity between Frederick and Edith developed into a passionate love affair. At first Percy seemed somewhat indifferent to the turn of events. Perhaps he hoped as do some betrayed spouses, that this was a passing affair which would soon burn itself out. When it became plain that this was not to be he ordered Bywaters out of his home where the former had been residing. The result was that the guilty pair began a series of clandestine meetings whenever Bywaters was home from sea.

Matters culminated when on the night of October 3/4 1922, while the Thompsons were on their way home from the theatre and were walking from Ilford Station along the Belgrave Road towards Kensington Gardens, Bywaters ran up behind them and stabbed Percy Thomson to death. Although Edith's account was initially that the murderer was a stranger, it became clear that she had been aware that the assassin was Bywaters and that her story was an attempt to shield her lover. Nevertheless there was no evidence that she was, though present, aiding and abetting the killer which was the charge against her when she was brought to trial. Indeed such evidence as there was went the other way since a witness who lived near the site of the crime heard her cry, "Don't, oh don't".

There was no other testimony at that stage which could possibly satisfy a jury that she had cooperated with Bywaters in the crime. Sir Travers Humphreys, a junior counsel for the defence at the trial, writes in his book, *A Book of Trials*:

> "In legal phraseology, mere knowledge that a crime is being committed is not enough to establish the offence of aiding and abetting. Now of direct evidence that Mrs Thompson was assisting Bywaters, there was absolutely none. There was an equal absence of direct proof that she knew the assault was to be made in that place or at that time."

Humphreys continues, however, "I should have thought it my duty to ask for the decision of the law officers of the Crown as to whether the charge of murder ought to proceed against her, but for one piece of evidence unprecedented in its character so far as my knowledge went, and dreadful in its significance, seeing the nature of the charge against her". Here Humphrey's is referring to the letters written by Edith to Frederick during their affair and which the latter had foolishly kept. These letters which we shall consider in depth, on their face value, showed clearly that Edith was discussing the possible method of killing her husband. As such they were disastrous for the chances of acquittal which without them should have been inevitable.

Nevertheless this author will contend that even with the letters in evidence the case for the prosecution that Edith Thompson was aiding and abetting the murder of her husband was not substantiated.

Only a minority of the letters were exhibited, and that in a haphazard manner. Some were excluded for absurd reasons. Those which were relied upon by the Crown as showing guilt were not taken in context with the others.

Secondly and most importantly, the indictment was "principal in the second degree". There might have been a stronger case on the crimes of accessory before the fact or conspiracy, but these charges were not proceeded with. The jury failed to give effect to, or the judge sufficiently to emphasise, the significance of Edith's cries of protest at the time of the murder or her distress immediately afterwards. To suggest that these were affectation was surely preposterous.

The fact of her meeting with Bywaters earlier on the day of the murder did not help her cause, but there was certainly no evidence that she had agreed with him the time and place of the killing. As she had already let it be known that she was going to the theatre with her husband that evening, it is not surprising that she realised Bywaters was the killer. The evidence fell well short of establishing she knew he was carrying a knife or that he intended to kill Percy on that fateful night.

The cry of protest which came from Edith was posited by the judge as inconsistent with her account as given to the police and later to the court. But this assumption is not fully justified neither is the inference that because Edith said things that were not true that means that she was a party to the stabbing. An inference may be legitimately drawn on the basis of other facts, but a mere presumption is not admissible in our law of evidence. If the two are confused the danger is that the burden of proof shifts to the defence—which it never should.

The case of William Joyce was of a completely different kind. There was little dispute regarding the facts. It was the law of treason which was the centrepiece of this particular drama. It is a fundamental principle of the British Constitution that Parliament makes the law and the judiciary applies it. But it is the task of the judges to implement the variety of legal rules to an equally infinite number of situations which arise in human affairs. When this occurs they may sometimes extend the previously understood and accepted meaning of a well-established piece of legislation. This is what is occasionally called "judge made law".

If this position is allowed to stand it remains the law of the nation. If however Parliament considers that the judge concerned or the judges jointly have acted wrongly it will pass amending legislation which alters what it regards as an incorrect interpretation of the law as it stood.

It must be plainly stated that in the case of William Joyce the extension of the law of treason by the then highest court in the land, the Judicial Committee of the House of Lords, stands unaltered by subsequent Act of Parliament, and therefore such criticism as is made, can only at the most be on the basis that that court's decision does not appear to be reasonable or consistent with previous recognised principles of the law of treason in this country.

A further point which should be emphasised is that there is no argument whatever that can be advanced on behalf of Joyce on the merits. Joyce was a wholly despicable character. For 18 years he had lived with his parents and two successive wives in England. He received his education and employment here and professed great love for England as his home, yet he was unhesitatingly willing to betray the land for which he professed great affection. It was fortuitous that the many broadcasts that he made to this country from Nazi Germany came to be regarded with derision. The intention was to provoke alarm and dismay and so undermine the will of the British people to defeat the horrible tyranny of Nazidom.

Perhaps the crucial question about the Joyce case is this: "Did the High Court, the Court of Criminal Appeal and finally the House of Lords unjustifiably extend the law of treason in order to satisfy a popular sentiment at the end of the Second World War that Joyce, having been captured, must not be allowed to escape from the consequences of his five years of treachery?"

When the prosecution of Joyce began at the Central Criminal Court in September 1945, the Crown immediately ran into what threatened to be a difficulty: it had always been a cardinal element of the law of treason that English law had no jurisdiction to try an offence committed abroad by an alien, although a British subject is triable in our courts for such a crime committed anywhere in the world. This precept is consistent with both law and common sense. Were it not so a Frenchman who has committed a crime in New York would be triable in London.

Enquiries revealed, to the consternation of the prosecuting authorities that Joyce was not a British citizen. Joyce had been born on the 24 April

1906 in Brooklyn New York. His father Michael Francis Joyce married in New York in May 1905; in 1894 he became a naturalised American citizen.

In 1922 the Joyce family, having lived in Ireland, County Mayo, came to England where William grew up. He studied at Battersea Polytechnic and Birkbeck College where he graduated in 1927. From 1928 to 1930 he was active as a helper to the Conservative Party, then studied psychology at Kings College, London.

On 4 July 1933 he illegally obtained a British passport—being a foreigner—which was issued to him for a period of five years. On his application this was renewed for one year. His application for renewal was on 24 August 1939. Joyce and his wife went to Germany in August. On 3 September Britain declared war on Germany.

In his introduction to the trial of William Joyce in the notable British Trials series J W Hall identifies the two issues involved:

> "(1) Can any British court try an alien for a crime committed abroad (with the sole exception of piracy, which by the *Jus Gentium* has always been justifiable anywhere, on the basis that a pirate is an enemy of the human race, to be eliminated by whoever has the good fortune to catch him).
>
> (2) Assuming that there was jurisdiction to try him at all, did the fact that Joyce had applied for and obtained a British passport impose on him a duty of allegiance during its currency even when he was outside the British Dominions."

On these issues the courts decided against Joyce. Were they right to do so?

The third trial in which it is submitted that there was a miscarriage of justice is that of Timothy Evans.

The tragedy of Timothy Evans took place in January 1950. Evans was a Welshman of very retarded intellect which at the time of these events also lived at the home of the multiple murderer John Halliday Christie. This factor alone has much to do with what follows. Evans, largely in the basis of confessions he made was convicted of the murder of his daughter, although he had accused Christie of the murder of both his wife and daughter. Three years after Evans had been executed, Christie confessed to the murder of Mrs Evans. An official enquiry in 1966 found that Christie had also murdered the daughter. Evans was granted a posthumous pardon.

The essence of Evan's defence at his trial was that Christie had murdered Geraldine, his daughter as well as Beryl his wife. Christie who gave evidence at the trial of Evans made strong denials to the defence allegation that he was the killer of both. He had a record of violence, but nothing was known then of his several murders of women, whose bodies were secreted at the home of both Christie and Evans: No. 10 Rillington Place.

During the trial alibi witnesses were called for Evans who had no criminal convictions, but were unavailing, Evans withdrew his confession, but had fatally undermined his credibility by his tendency to make contradictory statements. The judge, Mr Justice Lewis, seemed prejudicial against Evans and his summing-up was unfavourable to the defence. An appeal failed.

There is little doubt that Evans was unjustly convicted and executed.

PART 1
EDITH JESSIE THOMPSON

Three Cases that Shook the Law

CHAPTER 1

The Background Story

If there is one thing which impresses about the background of Edith Jessie Thompson, the central figure of the tragic story which follows, it is its sheer normality. It not infrequently occurs that people who ultimately are led by their destiny into being charged with terrible crimes have, to say the least, a discouraging or gravely disadvantaged start in life. Sometimes the environment in which they have grown up is steeped in criminality. Frequently they have had the type of parents who set their offspring a bad example. Or they have been emotionally damaged by a lack of love or affection. Only in comparatively recent years has psychology revealed how children who have been denied adequate care and devotion themselves grow up to be lacking in warmth and tenderness.

In the case of Edith Thompson the reverse is true. From the time of her birth on Monday 25 December 1893, when she was christened Edith Jessie, she received all the cherishing a child could want. This fondness from the family, which came to include her younger sister Avis, together with three brothers, was to continue throughout her short life until her terrible end.

For the very early part of her life Edith lived in the modest but comfortable home at 231 Shakespeare Crescent in Manor Park. This was a terraced house in which Edith and Avis shared a room. The home had a small garden in which the children could play, by no means a universal amenity in those days, and at that level of society.

As a schoolgirl all reports indicate that Edith was vivacious, attractive and extrovert. She made friends easily and joined in activities of the kind familiar to young children in their schooldays. Sometimes trips were organized to places of interest in London or to Wanstead Park. Edith, moreover, was a mentally bright child. She enjoyed reading and displayed skill in the composition of essays. Acting in school plays and dancing were among her accomplishments.

In the house she assisted her mother in bringing up her three brothers. At the age of 16 Edith was employed by a firm of clothing manufacturers in East London. She worked as a junior clerk. She then moved to a firm of cardboard manufacturers in Southwark. In 1910 she became a book-keeper with Louis London, wholesale clothing manufacturers near Aldgate Station, and more permanently in 1911 commenced employment with Carlton & Prior wholesale milliners on the north side of Barbican. There she greatly impressed her superiors with both her personality and competence. She remained with this firm for the rest of her life, ultimately rising to be chief buyer.

The Marriage of Percy and Edith

Edith Graydon met Percy Thompson when he was 18 and she was 15. The actual course of events which finally led to their marriage in January 1916, some six years later, remains a little obscure, but so far as Edith is concerned two things are obvious. The first is that she married too young for someone of her personality and temperament, and secondly the pair were plainly unsuited. These factors provided fertile ground for trouble when the good looking Freddy Bywaters came into the picture. Little is known about how Edith and Percy became acquainted in the first place. The young girl book-keeper was flattered by the attention of the older man, who was well-dressed and had steady employment. They had certain interests in common, such as music and amateur theatricals.

After a long courtship Percy and Edith were married in 1916. Prior to the marriage Edith had become chief buyer for Carlton & Prior, earning a salary in excess of that received by her fiancé. Thus it is clear that from the start of their marriage Edith and Percy would retain their respective employments. Edith had shown no enthusiasm for starting a family, and the joint income enabled the pair to live in some comfort and enjoy entertainments together. They settled in the then fashionable town of Ilford. The signs were good. But they were not as good as they must have appeared to those who knew them at the time.

What is the secret of a happy marriage? The question is as old as humanity. Many have attempted to supply an answer. There is none. We may bear in mind the words of *The Rubaiyat of Omar Khayyam*,

> "Myself when young did eagerly frequent, doctor and saint, and heard great argument about it, and about but evermore came out by the same door as in I went."

There is no answer. But one thing is certain: if the pair are not well suited to each other the marriage has far less chance of being successful. Percy Thompson had admired his new wife's personality and intelligence. The possibility that he might not be able to satisfy them never occurred to him. How does a steady, unadventurous prosaic husband satisfy a flighty, volatile capricious wife? How does he escape an attitude of mind on her part that she is tied to a dull fellow who has nothing more to offer than an uneventful existence, a humdrum repetitious life without sparkle or fun? It is a tragedy of human relationships as immemorial as human life itself.

Percy and Edith were completely incompatible, and they lived in a society which did not recognise such problems. Marriage was marriage and that was that. The sacred bond of matrimony was about home and children. The question of the happiness of the husband and wife came a very definite second—if then. Divorce was only available on very limited grounds, and in any event the upheaval and expense involved was a great deterrent to the majority of people.

Perhaps it was an ill omen when, on the 16 January 1916, the day when Percy and Edith married, the latter expressed severe doubts about going through with it. She protested to her father that she did not want to go to the church for the ceremony, and only his reassurances persuaded her to do so.

The marriage went well for a while—as they usually do. After the honeymoon the pair lived at 231 Shakespeare Crescent. Percy was enlisted into the army, but after a short time was discharged as physically unfit.

Edith was pleased that she had no reason to fear being a war widow, but the obvious pleasure which Percy displayed on escaping military service did not make him a more admirable figure in her sight.

Having decided to live in Ilford the Thompsons in due course purchased 41 Kensington Gardens, an eight room Victorian property, very comfortable for two people. Edith showed no enthusiasm whatever for starting a family. With both parties earning they had a joint income which enabled them to enjoy their interests and pastimes, in particular the theatre. The war was over and life was returning to normal. Their future should have been assured. But already the basic incompatibility between the two had begun to show itself.

The fact that both parties had separate occupations took them apart for most days of the week. They both left home at an early hour, but Percy who was a conscientious and industrious employee was frequently delayed late at work while going through his accounts. Edith, who had been promoted to manageress at Carlton & Prior began to build her own social and professional circle, as is the way with a career woman, and no doubt met and associated with men who were more stimulating company than her prosaic husband. Arguments began between the two. In particular his suggestion of starting a family was swept aside by Edith. Occasionally there were violent incidents.

Into this rapidly failing marriage came the youthful Frederick Bywaters. There are two myths regarding the Thompson and Bywaters case which should be disposed of without delay. The first is that Bywaters was an innocent young man seduced by an older woman. The second was that a happy marriage was wrecked by a wicked ruthless adulterer.

In his book on the trial in the *Notable British Trials* series Filson Young sums up the characters of Edith and Freddie admirably.

> "It is when we come to the characters of Bywaters and Mrs Thompson that we are at once confronted with an element of the unusual. Neither of these persons was at all like what the general public thinks. Bywaters was not the innocent young lad that his defenders presented to the jury; Edith Thompson was not the corrupt, sorceress portrayed by the prosecution. A great deal of play was made about their respective ages, and it was suggested

that she was an experienced woman corrupting a young lad. That is not the way I see it. Bywaters was twenty and she was twenty eight, but in some ways he was the older of the two, as he was certainly the more masterful. He was an almost excessively virile animal type. He had knocked about the world. He had knowledge of life, and an exceptionally strong will. You will read in the course of the trial a great deal about the woman's influence upon him, but I am convinced that his influence upon her was at least as strong as hers upon him, and they came upon their undoing because of an exaggerated difference between them. Bywaters as I read his character, was totally devoid of imagination; actions were his only realities. Edith Thompson had an excess of imagination. To her actions were unimportant. Her chief consciousness was hardly even in what she was doing at the time, but in a world of dream and make believe. If this aspect of the characters of the two people concerned be kept in mind, I think it will make things clear which must otherwise remain obscure."

In his book *The Innocence of Edith Thompson* Lewis Broad says of Bywaters:

"We can see him more clearly — not a champion in our eyes, but an immature young man, of no particular distinction, save that he had a strange look about his eyes, giving a compelling quality to his glances — hypnotic quality, perhaps to the women who received them. There was nothing about young Bywaters to suggest he would be other than a sober and industrious citizen. His record was impeccable. He left school with a good character and excellent reports. At sea his early reputation was confirmed. At the end of each voyage his certificate of discharge credited him with good character and ability."

Broad continues by explaining that Bywaters, who had sailed pretty well all over the world before he was 20-years-old was much loved by his mother, a woman who, in her widowhood — her husband had been killed in the war — had started a milliners business in Norwood. Here the son had acquired a background that made for understanding with the vivacious manageress of the milliners established in the city. "So too there was a common interest between Thompson the shipping clerk, and the young man who was clerk aboard ships of the P & O Company."

The Road to Murder

One of the remarkable features of the Thompson Bywaters case is the failure of Percy Thompson to recognise the growing affair between Bywaters and his wife. At the start of their friendship Percy Thompson took a liking to young Freddie. Like many a trusting husband, he failed to see the early danger signs. Bywaters was twenty and attractive to women due to his good looks and adventurous lifestyle. Edith was twenty eight, romantic and perhaps a little envious of the type of young women of the twenties who flouted convention, and not uncommonly, morals. Due to the terrible carnage at the front in the Great War single girls found it much easier to find jobs, and hence lead their own lives than had been the case with an earlier generation of women. There was a spirit abroad of what in the 1960s became known as "women's lib". In addition Edith was finding life with an unadventurous older husband somewhat "hum-drum".

The light which lit the fire was a vacation which all three made to the Isle of Wight in June 1921. It was there that Edith and Freddie had their first kiss. It was there that they realised that they had fallen in love.

By this time Bywaters, who had regularly visited the Thompsons at their home at 41 Kensington Gardens, was now their lodger. Still Percy was ignorant of the developing catastrophe for his marriage.

It would be unjust to blame Percy for naïvely in failing to grasp the situation earlier. This view can come dangerously close to transferring responsibility from the villain to the victim. Perhaps, as was the prevailing culture at the time, he had already realised that his marriage was not as satisfactory as it might have been, but nevertheless thought that this was not an uncommon condition in matrimony and that he and Edith should and would work to preserve their union. Moreover he trusted his wife not to betray him — a trust which proved to be sadly misplaced.

Meanwhile Edith was feeding her aching romanticism with sentimental and passionate novels and visits to the theatre to watch *avant-garde* plays. During the trip to the Isle of Wight Edith's attraction to Bywaters increased due to his predilection for swimming, an activity which Percy avoided, and his ability to hold his alcohol which was not shared by Percy who arrived home after a boozy session with Freddie much the worse for wear.

After the Isle of Wight holiday Percy invited Freddie to become a lodger. The alacrity with which both Edith and Bywaters accepted this invitation should surely have been a danger signal for Percy—but it seems not to have been.

By now in June 1921 Edith began confiding in Bywaters regarding her marriage to Percy. Her boredom, her lack of feeling for him—in short that she was not in love with her husband. There is no more open invitation that a wife can offer a predatory paramour.

The *ménage a trois* which settled down at 41 Kensington Gardens in July 1921 looked innocent enough—but only to the casual observer. During what might have been a temporary stay by Freddie he and Edith became lovers and would so remain to the end of their story. Freddie then became a paying lodger and a situation was created which could not endure. For Edith, increasingly besotted with her young lover, Percy became an encumbrance. He was a nuisance who stood between them. He had become for her a tiresome bore. A wife, her young lover and an older husband. The circumstances are classic—and by no means uncommon—as the judge pointed out at the trial.

Pictures of the time tell a vivid story? One, taken before Bywaters came on the scene, shows a laughing group of six people. In the centre is Percy looking happy and ebullient. In front of him is Edith, smiling but more cautiously. Another of a threesome taken at Southsea on 11 June 1921 displays a smiling Percy, an unsmiling Edith and a Frederick with his head cradled by Edith's right hand in her hip. Others tell a very different story. Taken in the garden of 41 Kensington Gardens on 10 July they depict a sullen, solemn-faced Percy seated between a bored and miserable looking Edith and her brother Newneham. In another, looking listless and discontented, she is the central figure on either side Frederick and Percy, the former reading a book and the latter perusing a newspaper.

Finally there is a photo of 3 September 1922 of Percy and Edith in their garden only a month before his murder. Edith is seated and looking meek and shame-faced. Percy, standing behind her exhibits a look almost of defiance as if to say, "She is mine and will remain so."

From the beginning of July tension mounted in the Thompson household. Percy was unaware that his wife and Bywaters were already lovers. But he sensed a growing coldness towards him on her part. He made an effort to put things right with her—but it was a non-starter. Already she found his presence repellent. His suggestion of starting a family is dismissed immediately. He knows by now that the two have started going out together. Percy discussed separation with Edith, but somewhat surprisingly this idea comes to nothing.

Then, on Monday the 1 August matters come to a head. There is a quarrel between Percy and Edith, Edith suffers a bruised arm when violence occurs. An angry Bywaters intervenes on her behalf and the disturbance ends with Percy ordering Frederick out of the house. On 5 August Bywaters left. From now on the affair was continued by means of a series of clandestine meetings and letters.

One thing is certain, Percy's marriage was, in all but a legal sense, finished. Yet he failed to recognise this. Had he done so and taken the necessary steps to end it three lives could have been saved. Was he so proud and stubborn that he refused to believe he had lost Edith to a much younger man? Or did he hope that this was a passing fantasy on his wife's part that would soon "blow over."

A strange feature of the situation is that Edith herself showed no enthusiasm for divorce. Although in the letters, she declared her undying love for Frederick and for longing to be alone with him permanently, she shrank from taking any positive steps to end her marriage to Percy. Did she behind her extravagantly romantic pronouncements, harbour some secret doubts about what marriage to Frederick would be like. A young husband, eight years below her own age, away at sea most of the time. A man who was attractive to women and who had already caused her some concern regarding a woman in Australia. And what would her own position be? Probably she would lose her steady and gainful employment for a man who had little to offer in respect of security.

Passion is an adventure, marriage is not. Perhaps she foresaw in a future with Bywaters a fragile bond which might end with her losing both her lover and her husband.

After Bywaters departure on 5 August the clandestine meetings — and the letters began.

It is commonly acknowledged that without the letters there would have been no case against Edith Thompson. With incredible folly Bywaters kept the letters which she had written to him and thus ensured that she would suffer the same fate as himself.

At the trial the Crown put in evidence those letters which they maintained clearly disclosed a wish and an intention of Edith that her husband be murdered.

Two things must be born in mind. Firstly, only a minor portion were produced before the court in comparison with the majority which were not. Secondly, and crucially, the indictment which was proceeded with charged Edith with being a principal in the second degree, namely being present aiding and abetting the murder of Percy by Frederick Bywaters. The second indictment which contained charges of conspiracy to murder, soliciting and inciting to commit murder and administering poison and administering a destructive thing with intent to murder were not proceeded with.

Therefore the issue for the jury was not: "What was the state of mind of Edith when she wrote the correspondence to Bywaters?" but "Do the contents of the letters produced prove beyond reasonable doubt that she aided and abetted her lover in the murder of her husband in the 4 October 1922?" In other words, are the letters sufficient evidence to show that Edith Thompson participated in the crime committed on the 4 October 1922?

The question of the correspondence between Edith and Freddie we shall consider in more details when we come to the trial. Suffice to say at this point there are many reasons to suppose, as was the contention of Sir Henry Curtis-Bennett, that Edith was fantasising about ways of killing her husband rather than seriously encompassing his demise.

The two methods of assassination which she allegedly proposed were broken glass and poison. The absurdity of the former soon becomes obvious. Is it conceivable that Percy would not have seen fragments of broken light bulb in his food? And is it possible that having done so he would not immediately suspect Edith, and challenge her on the subject?

With regards to poison — it is plain that Edith had no knowledge of the subject whatsoever. There is no evidence at all that she tried to obtain dangerous chemicals, or from whom. She clearly had no idea which quantities would prove lethal — if in fact she ever administered any. Her accounts of Percy finding that his tea tasted strange are melodramatic and laughable. These factors coupled with the clear tone of her writings which indicates, as she feared, that her lover was unmistakably cooling off, support Curtis-Bennett's submission that here was a foolish love-sick woman desperate to impress her less than reliable paramour.

The Letters

If ever anyone on trial for murder brought about their own conviction and execution that person was Edith Thompson. Her letters were the only evidence of a guilty intent — namely the alleged incitement of Bywaters to murder her husband — and for that reason, as we shall see, the prosecuting counsel made the very most of them.

Only a minority of the letters contained words in which it would be difficult, if not impossible, to argue that Edith did not have the demise of her husband in mind. We shall see how, at the trials, the Solicitor-General, Sir Thomas Inskip presented them to the jury. One thing all the letters disclose, and that is the wild obsessive passion which Edith felt for her lover. As the song goes: "Maybe that love is blind when passion rules." Passion rules with the power of a tyrant in this particular romance. The circumstances brought another old adage into effect: "Distance makes the heart grow fonder." Never was a love affair conducted from such distances and with so many interruptions.

If we scan the whole period of the letters from Edith to Bywaters from September 1921 to August 1922 the absence of Bywaters on the high seas fills a very large part of the time. On the 9 September 1921 Bywaters left England on his ship *The Morea* as a laundry steward, returning on the 29 October of that year. On December 11 he sailed again coming back on the 6 January. Once again he left on 20 January and returned on the 25 May. Finally having departed on June 9 he is home again on 23 September and goes to live at his mother's house.

Through all of this time the correspondence continues with the passion in Edith's dispatches undimmed. Some of her earlier missives are ambiguous in their meaning, but later when the references to poison and broken glass appear it would be very difficult to argue that Mrs Thompson did not want her husband dead—even if she was fantasising rather than making a firm statement of intent. One of the strangest features of a story, which has many unusual aspects, is the question of why the lovers, in view of the intensity of their passion, didn't elope. Some of Edith's letters to Freddie seem to hint at the classic solution of a mutual suicide pact—though it seems doubtful whether this would have appealed to him. It is true that at that period divorce carried a much greater stigma than it does today and the grounds in law for such a course were fewer than is the case now. Nevertheless it seems extraordinary that apart from expressions of longing for a day when they can be together nothing of a practical nature appears in Edith's correspondence to bring this about.

Edith was young and attractive. She was thought highly of by her employers and received a salary above the average. As a pair the two enjoyed an income which was adequate for their support. If they had simply set up home together Percy would in time, have had little choice but to divorce his wife. Instead, however, of a sensible although less than moral arrangement of this kind, we find absurd suggestions of feeding Percy with glass or poison which over time will render him sick, but without any certainty of effectively killing him and in any event might easily be traced to the perpetrators. As long before the fatal day as November 1921 Frederick and Percy had discussed the question of Edith and her husband being divorced. Bywaters asked Thompson if he would set Edith free by means of divorce or separation, but at first Percy seemed to be undecided. When Bywaters commented that he was making her life hell, Thompson replied sharply: "Well, I have got her and I will keep her. I don't see that this concerns you." The significant features of this conversation are that Bywaters did not clarify the fact that it would be for his benefit that the marriage would be dissolved, nor did Percy seem to grasp the full consequence for himself of the developing situation.

In his work *Verdict in Dispute* the great crime writer Edgar Lustgarten points out the way in which a preconceived theory regarding the letters can be used as a blanket explanation of them all:

> "Though other extracts gained equal prominence at the trial, one surmises that in the initial phase these furnished the key. They laid a firm-looking foundation for a practicable theory which was confidently applied to unriddle ambiguities. By the aid of this explanatory touchstone, each could be resolved to favour the Crown's case."

For instance:

> "This time really will be the last you go away like things are wont it? We said it before darlint I know and we failed, but there will be no failure this next time darlint, there mustn't be. I'm telling you if things are the same again then I am going to visit you wherever it is. If it's to sea I am coming too and if it's nowhere I'm also coming darlint. You'll never leave me behind again, never unless things are different."

What did Mrs Thompson mean, "unless things are different"? Obvious said the Crown: She meant "unless we have done the murder."

"I ask you again to think out all the plans and methods for me."

What did "plans and methods?" mean. "Obvious," said the Crown; she meant "ways and means of murder."

> "Yes darlint, you are jealous of him but I want you to be, he has the right by law that all that you have the right to by nature and by love, yes darlint be jealous, so much that you will do something desperate."

What did Mrs Thompson mean — "Do something desperate?"

"Obvious" said the Crown, "she meant brace yourself for murder."

If some of these inferences seem prejudiced or forced this must be said in fairness to the Crown, make one assumption and it is true that all else follows. If what one terms the key passages are taken at face value, if every statement in them is taken as a fact, each of the incidents described by Mrs Thompson is assumed to have occurred exactly as she says, then there can only be one possible conclusion. Mrs Thompson had herself tried to kill her husband and had been imploring Bywaters to succeed where she had failed.

> "That was the conclusion granted the assumption. But was the assumption justified that Mrs Thompson never indulged in flights of fancy and that all her reporting was meticulously exact? The trial, so far as she was concerned, became a committee of enquiry to decide this single point."

Three Cases that Shook the Law

CHAPTER 2

The Murder of Percy Thompson

On the 23 September 1922 Bywaters' ship *The Morea* arrived at Tilbury. Once again he is home, but this time a series of events commences which ends in murder. Edith is extremely anxious to make contact with Freddie. Her ardour has not lessened in the slightest degree. She telephones him twice at his mother's address and the two recommence their meetings.

Earlier Edith had used guile to retain the loyalty of her lover. She did this by the pretence that she was co-operating in the murder of her husband by the use of poison and broken glass. She also attempted to arouse his jealousy by the deception that the physical side of sex had not entirely finished with her husband. She used expressions such as "darlint I've surrendered to him unconditionally now—do you understand me?", "I am giving all, the dutiful wife and accepting everything." She was even frank enough to write, "Yes darlint you are jealous of him but I want you to be… Yes darlint be jealous so much that you will do something desperate."

These foolish, irresponsible messages were found to have a most provocative effect on an impressionable and proud young man. They were careless and thoughtless words used by a reckless and self-obsessed young woman. Her counsel would have served her cause better by presenting her as such to the jury rather than as a victim of a great and beautiful love—a romantic fable which irritated the jury and alienated the judge.

In an undated letter written shortly before the murder, Edith waxes almost poetic regarding the time spent with Freddie on a Friday before the murder of Percy:

"Darlingest lover of mine, thank you, thank you oh thank you a thousand times for Friday—it was lovely—it's always lovely to go out with you.

And then Saturday—yes I did feel happy—I didn't think a teeny bit about anything in this world, except being with you—and all Saturday evening I was thinking about you—I was just with you, in a big arm chair in front of a great big fire feeling all the time how much I had won—cos I have darlint won such a lot—it feels such a great big thing to me sometimes—that I can't breathe.

When you are away and I see girls with men walking along together—perhaps they are acknowledged as sweethearts—they look so ordinary then I feel proud—so proud to think and feel that you are my lover and even though not acknowledged I can still hold you—just with a tiny hope.

Darlint, we've said we'll be pals haven't we, shall we say we'll always be lovers—even though secret ones, or is it (this great big love) a thing we can't control—dare we say that—I think I will dare, yes I will, I'll always love you—if you are dead—if you have left me even if you don't still love me, I shall always you.

Your love to me is new, it is something different, it is my life and if things should go badly wrong with us, I shall always have this past year to look back upon and feel that 'then I lived'. I never did before and I never shall again.

Darlingest lover, what happened last night? I don't know myself. I only know how I felt—no, not really how I felt but how I could feel—if time and circumstances were different. It seems like a great welling up of love—of feeling of inertia just as if I was in your hands to do with as you will and I feel that if you do as you wish I shall be happy, it's physical purely as I can't really describe it—but you will understand darlint won't you? You said you knew it would be like this one day—if it hadn't would you have been disappointed? Darlingest when you are rough, I go dead—try not to be please."

There is then a passage regarding a book which he has given her.

"I tried so hard to find a way out of tonight darlingest but he was suspicious and still is—I suppose we must make a study of this deceit for some time longer. I hate it, I hate every lie I have to tell to see you—because lies seem such small mean things to attain such an object as ours. We ought to be able to use great big things for great big love like ours. I'd love to be able to say 'I am going to see my lover tonight'. If I did he would prevent me—there would be scenes and he would come to 168 and interfere and I couldn't bear that—I could be beaten all over at home and still be defiant—but at 168 it's different. It's my living—you wouldn't want me to live on him would you, and I shouldn't want to—darlint it's funds that are our stumbling block—until we have those we can do nothing. Darlingest, find me a job abroad, I'll go tomorrow and not say I was going to a soul and not have one little regret. I said I wouldn't think—that I'd try to forget—circumstances pal, help me to forget again—I have succeeded up to now—but it's thinking of tonight and tomorrow when I can't see you and feel you holding me.

Darlint do something tomorrow night will you? Something to make you forget. I'll be hurt I know, but I want you to hurt me—I do really—the bargain now seems so one sided—so unfair—but how can I alter it?"

There then follows a passage regarding a watch which she had given to him that includes these two baffling phrases: "He's still well—he's going to gaze all day long at you in your temporary home—after Wednesday."

"Don't forget what we talked about in the Tea Room. I'll still risk and try if you will—we only have 3¾ years left darlint. Try and help please."

The whole scenario of the events leading up to the murder of Percy Thompson contradict rather than support the thesis that the crime was arranged by Edith and Freddie and accomplished with the cooperation of both. We have to examine this bearing in mind that she was charged with being present, aiding and abetting the action of Bywaters.

On this issue the letter quoted from above is extremely important since it is the final one sent by Edith to Frederick before her husband is killed. There is nothing whatever in that letter which expressly or even by implication suggests a conspiracy by these two to murder Thompson. The whole tone of the letter, expressed in the passionate terms which permeated most of the letters, relates to the future. Let us examine some of the phrases.

"I tried so hard to find a way out of tonight darlingest, but he was suspicious and still is—I suppose we must make a study of this deceit for some time longer." Why, if she had planned with Bywaters to murder her husband in a day or two's time, do we find her trying to get out of the trip to the theatre with Percy which was the alleged strategy for his assassination? Why should she write, "I suppose we must make a study of this deceit for some time longer," if so far as the plotters were concerned there was to be "no time longer"?

"Darlingest find me a job abroad. I'll go tomorrow and not say I was going to a soul and not have one little regret." Why, if she was planning the killing of Percy with Frederick should Edith be writing about finding employment abroad?

"I'll go tomorrow and not say I was going to a soul and not have one little regret." What happened to the new life together they are alleged to have planned if Edith was expressing a desire to go away alone?

Even the passage of which the prosecution made so much is ambivalent. "Darlint, do something tomorrow night will you to make you forget. I'll be hurt I know, but I want you to hurt me—I do really—the bargain now—seems so one sided—so unfair, but how can I alter it?" What these words mean is surely incomprehensible. What would make Bywaters forget? What is the bargain which seems to be one sided and so unfair? Without further enlightenment it is anyone's guess.

Finally we have the ultimate passage: "Don't forget what we talked about in the Tea Room, I'll still risk and try if you will—we only have 3 ¾ years left darlingest, try and help."

Sir Thomas Inskip dealt with this matter very briefly: "I ask what did they talk about in the Tea Room? I put it that there was a long course of suggestion resulting from a desire to escape from the position, and a fresh suggestion was made in the Tea Room."

The suggestion, or rather the implication put forward by the Solicitor-General appears to emanate from his own imagination rather than from any item of evidence. In his summing-up to the jury the judge goes even further in constructing a conversation of which there is no evidence whatever that it occurred:

> "Then we came to the last letter at the end of September, exhibit 60. It is quite obvious that that bit refers to a meeting which was fully answered, and much more point was made of it. It is no point in the case now. 'Do not forget what we talked of in the Tea Room: I will still risk and try if you will'. And it is said it is poison or it is the dagger. 'We have got many things to consider; shall we run away if we can get the money or shall we try poison? We will talk it over.'"

Exhibit 60 is fully and faithfully produced in *Appendix 1*, in *Notable British Trials*.

There is no mention in that letter of poison or a dagger. By putting into the minds of the jury the likelihood of such things being discussed by the defendants when there was no evidence whatever of the subject Mr Justice Shearman was guilty of a serious misdirection which might have influenced their decision. It is surprising that Sir Henry Curtis-Bennett made no objection.

If one follows the movements of the parties concerned up to the moment of the murder these indicate no signs whatever of a planned assassination. What they show is an angry, jealous and resentful Bywaters. A proud and possessive young man relegated to the side lines while to his frustration Edith is enjoying an evening at the theatre with the husband he has come to loathe. In *The Innocence of Edith Thompson* Lewis Broad writes:

> "So, on that Tuesday evening he [Bywaters] was left by himself while the man with the rights, the husband in possession, escorted her to the theatre, he was left to the mercy of all the accumulated devils of his hours

of brooding. You can imagine him spending the evening with her people, the Graydons of Manor Park. He was there in the flesh chatting away, to outward appearances a normal young man idling away an evening of his leave. But his thoughts were elsewhere, on the woman enjoying herself in the company of the husband in possession, while he was in the possession of the ten thousand devils of his hours of brooding. The man with the rights—the jealous lover saw something other than that, something several degrees lower than a snake. The hours of the evening went slowly, but they went the way of other hours. At eleven o'clock the young man left the family circle and went off into the night."

All the events leading up to and including the murder point to the conclusion that Bywaters was acting independently and without the planning or cooperation of Edith Thompson. This is what he maintained at the trial and there is little reason to doubt it. Bywaters was familiar with the route home which the Thompsons would take and the approximate time of their presence there after leaving the theatre.

The issue is not how well Bywaters knew the route home taken by Edith and Percy—it is: "Is there any convincing evidence that when Bywaters overtook them he did so by arrangement with Edith?" There is no such evidence.

Bywaters made it clear at the trial in his evidence in chief that he routinely carried a knife which inflicted the injuries on Thompson:

> **Cecil Whiteley:** "Were you carrying your knife when you went there (to the Graydons)?"
> **Frederick Bywaters:** "I was."
> **Whiteley:** "Did you carry that knife everywhere while in England?"
> **Bywaters:** "Yes"
> **Whiteley:** "Did you ever use it for anything?"
> **Bywaters:** "Cutting string or cutting things handy."
> **Whiteley:** "Is that the purpose for which you carried it?"
> **Bywaters:** "I thought that it might be handy at any time."
> **Whiteley:** "A knife that size and character?"
> **Bywaters:** "Yes, Handy at sea"

Whiteley: "Handy at sea: But was it handy at home?"
Bywaters: "Yes."

Any suggestion by the prosecution that Bywaters had purchased his knife shortly before the murder in order to kill Thompson is rendered pure assumption by the fact that no enquiry was made of Osborne and Co of Aldersgate Street where the knife was obtained.

There is no mention of such a weapon in any of the letters and the fact that the modus operandi proposed, if proposed it was, was poison makes it unlikely that Edith would have envisaged such a violent stabbing in the street as the proper method of despatching Percy.

If Edith and Freddie had seriously intended to slay Percy they had the whole of the time from the incriminating letters in April until October to lay their plans. They had ample opportunity to do so during the penultimate visit home by Freddie between May 25 and June 9 1922.

On the night of October 3rd to 4th Frederick was near to the commencement of his next voyage. He was consumed with jealousy that his beloved should be spending the final hours of his stay with the man who he now hated. The site of the murder was not especially dark and was only some 50 yards from the Thompson's home. Even at that late hour there were people about. Would Edith and her lover have chosen such a place for the terrible deed had they been working in conjunction? It would seem highly likely that strong words were exchanged between the two men before Bywaters drew his knife. Dr Percy James Drought, who conducted the post mortem examination on Thompson, gave evidence consistent with the initial assault having been conducted from the front:

> "With regard to the slight wound at the front, the assailant must have been in front and then got round to the back with the deeper ones. The stab that cut his carotid artery is more likely to have been struck from the back than from the front."

This would seem to support Bywaters account that the incident began with an argument over Edith and escalated into violence—although it provides Bywaters with no conceivable defence.

If the events, leading up to the Thompson murder favour Edith's case that she had not agreed with Bywaters on a plan to murder her husband, her subsequent behaviour more than supports her claim. John Webber, who lived at nearby 59 De Vere Gardens, Ilford was to give evidence at the trial that about 12.30 pm as he was going to retire to bed he head a woman's voice crying out, "Oh don't, oh don't". Cross-examined by Sir Henry Curtis-Bennett he said, "I have no doubt whatever that the voice I heard, 'Oh don't, oh don't' was the voice of Mrs Thompson". It is strange that more was not made of this crucial item of evidence by the defence at the trial. Stranger still is the manner in which the judge dealt with it in his summing-up:"There is one other very curious piece of evidence to which I want to call your attention, and that is the evidence of Mr Webber. He says he heard a noise, and these are his words, he heard these words 'Oh don't oh don't' in piteous tones. You know he is some way off, I am not saying it is true, it is for you to say whether it is accurate or whether it is imaginary, or whether he has made a mistake; but there is the evidence. The voice was Mrs Thompson's. 'It was three or four minutes before I came out, and then I heard the doctor ask had he been ill'. Now of course again it is for you to say, if you believe that, what the words mean 'oh don't oh don't' in piteous tones, and it is made use of by her counsel in showing that she objected to the murder and was saying 'don't'. Well a remark of force, but it is a double edged weapon. This evidence, if you think it is accurate, because if you think it means that when she saw him being stabbed or saw one of the stabs, she said 'don't, don't' it means she was looking on and she saw it all. The evidence is incompatible with the story that she was senseless and only recovered — you know her story, I need not go into that matter again — if she was pushed aside and damaged by a fall (and there is independent evidence that she had a bruise). That does not prove how the bruise was given, but her story is that she knew nothing of it. She saw some scuffling a little way down, and she saw the back of the man running away, knowing who he was.

"Of course, if that is so, it is impossible that she could be saying 'Don't, don't' and she saw the blows struck, I think it is entirely for you. I will not argue that. Of course you will bear in mind that if you think that is true, the fact that she was saying 'don't, don't' at the end of it would not protect her if she had summoned that man there and was only horrified when she saw the deed, and that he had compassed it. These are things that will appeal to you or anybody else; you will weigh them. But if you believe them you are in this difficulty, that it makes you disbelieve at once the whole of her evidence that she did not see it and indeed, if you think knowing what these wounds are like and what happened, it is almost incredible that she should not have seen what happened. It is a remarkable story for you to believe; that the sudden push against the wall rendered her senseless and stupefied. That is the story."

By the time of his summing-up the judge knew full well that Edith had admitted that she saw the two men scuffling together and that she knew that the assailant upon her husband was Bywaters. She explained the fact of her earlier false claim to know nothing about the attacker on the basis that she was trying to defend her lover from the consequences of his actions. This is a perfectly reasonable explanation. Her cry in the night, "Oh don't, oh don't" is perfectly consistent with her account given to the police after she had seen Bywaters in the library at the police station and had said, "Oh god, oh god, what can I do? Why did he do it? I did not want him to do it. I must tell the truth." It is also consistent with her evidence at the trial and with Bywaters own evidence. Yet this vital piece of testimony of John Webber is dismissed by the judge as "a very curious piece of evidence."

In dealing with it the judge's logic is flawed. He directed the jury that if the words were spoken they show that she saw the whole of the stabbing contrary to her story. This overlooks the fact that the evidence came from a witness who knew her voice and not from Edith Thompson herself. Moreover the words spoken while not coming from Edith's own testimony are consistent with her seeing a struggle going on. Yet Sir Montague Shearman said that they mean she saw Bywaters using the knife. This does not follow at all—except in the judge's unjustified assumption.

Detective Inspector Wensley who interviewed Edith shortly after the murder later wrote in a book dealing with this among other of his cases: "There was no doubt that her distress was genuine". This is entirely consistent with the evidence given at the trial by Dora Pittard, Percy Cleverly, Dr Maudslay and police sergeant Grimes, all of whom saw Edith Thompson immediately after the murder of her husband.

The prosecution, to maintain their proposition of guilt, were obliged to suggest to the jury that Edith, having planned the whole event with Bywaters, was now putting on a convincing act of being distraught and distressed. This is contrary to the view of at least six witnesses.

Nevertheless, it was the previous association with Bywaters and the discovery of Edith's letters to him which led to her arrest.

CHAPTER 3

The Trial: The Scene is Set

On Wednesday 6th December 1922 the Central Criminal Court in London, more commonly known as the Old Bailey, was crowded with onlookers. The case of the King against Bywaters and Thompson was already famous. This was long before what has become known as the "permissive society", and although the twenties were seen as a young generation in revolt against traditional and conventional morality, the rejection of these things was fairly muted by today's standards.

Here was a trial in which the prescribed behaviour in human society — illicit passion, adultery, conspiracy to murder and murder itself — was going to be fully exposed to the public gaze. Pornography and sexual explicitness was confined to grubby back street bookshops, and even that never went to the extremes of depravity available in recent years. The spectators in the public gallery of the court may attract some contempt for their appetite, but the explanation is no mystery.

In a criminal trial the search for the truth involves three parties: the judge, the jury and counsel, better known as barristers. Each has a separate function, each a different task and each a distinct responsibility. The judge is in charge of the conduct of the trial. This he or she must do with impartiality, although in the United Kingdom the judge is entitled to comment on the evidence as well as directing the jury on the law. Counsel's duty is to test the evidence by examination and cross-examination of witnesses and to assist the jury in their decision by their speeches at the end of the trial in favour of and against the accused person. Finally, the jury has the great responsibility of deciding the guilt or innocence of the defendant, who will, if convicted, be sentenced by the judge accordingly.

Lawyers on the continent of Europe who practise the inquisitorial system in which judges or assessors decide both fact and law regard our adversarial system as something of a "game".

Let us begin by considering the judge, Sir Montague Shearman. In his book *Criminal Justice: The True Story of Edith Thompson*, Rene Weis describes Mr Justice Shearman in the following terms:

> "The unreality of the place, the Old Bailey, is underlined by the alien look of the bewigged judiciary and the sphinx like figure of the trial judge sitting across the well of the court and facing the dock. Mr Justice Shearman, high churchman and stern moralist presides. A former athlete and the author of a book on football, he is a man of little intellectual distinction. He dislikes courtroom antics and disapproves of female jurors, whom he insists on addressing as 'gentlemen'.
>
> The most notable saying of this pillar of the community is that 'the court is not a theatre'. He is a family man of the old school. To him the ardent and intensely masculine looking young man opposite will only ever be the 'adulterer', the phrase he is to use again and again about Bywaters, particularly in his summing-up."

It is one thing to criticise Shearman's performance as judge in the Thompson-Bywaters trial, it is quite another to refer to him as "a man of little intellectual distinction." When a boy at Merchant Taylors School he won a scholarship to St John's College, Oxford. At Oxford he graduated with a first class degree in Classical Moderations and *Literae Humaniores*, commonly referred to as a "double first". This in itself was an outstanding academic and intellectual achievement. But to merge this with victory in the one hundred yards race at the Oxford and Cambridge University games in 1878 together with a rugby "blue" playing for Oxford University marks Montague Shearman out as a remarkable man.

Shearman was appointed a High Court judge in 1914. He presided over some notable trials of the period such as that of the solicitor Harold

The Trial: The Scene is Set

Greenwood in Wales in 1920 for murder by poisoning (Greenwood was acquitted) and those of Reginald Dunne and Joseph O'Sullivan the IRA assassins of General Wilson outside his house at 36 Eaton Place in 1922.

Shearman assembled a varied and impressive collection of contemporary art and, in sharp contrast, took a lifelong interest in football, regarding which he wrote several books. He retired in 1929 and died one year later.

The real question regarding the role of the judge in the Thompson and Bywaters trial is was it his view from the start of the case that both of the defendants were guilty and if so did he influence the jury to come to the verdict they reached—namely that both parties were in fact guilty?

It is the view of this author that the answer to both questions is in the affirmative. So far from being "a man of little intellectual distinction", Mr Justice Sherman was a very clever man. He was careful to pre-empt an appeal by giving an impeccable direction to the jury regarding their duties concerning the burden of proof and their function as distinct from his own. He was also justified in drawing their attention to the significance of the letters which Edith had written to her lover. But did he deal fully with the crucial point: even including the evidence of the letters was it established beyond reasonable doubt that Edith had planned with Bywaters the actual murder before the court and had she fully cooperated in its execution? If there was a real doubt about that, then the charge of principal in the second degree could and should not stand.

Leading counsel for the Crown was the Solicitor-General Sir Thomas Inskip. Inskip, during his long career in public life, occupied a variety of distinguished offices in both law and politics. Indeed it was a remarkable combination of both. He became a King's Counsel in 1914 and four years later he entered Parliament. In 1922, the year of the Thompson-Bywater trial, he was Solicitor-General following which, in 1928 he was made Attorney-General. Later in his career he became Lord Chancellor and Lord Chief Justice. He played a significant part in Church of England affairs. He died as Lord Caldecote, aged 71 in 1947.

As a lawyer-politician Inskip sometimes was obliged to leave the court to attend to his other duties. When he did so he left the Crown case in the hands of his juniors, Travers Humphreys and Roland Oliver. He had no need to fear. Travers Humphreys was recognised as one of the ablest advocates at the Bar. Richard Somers Travers Christmas Humphreys graduated at Cambridge in 1889 and was called to the Bar in the same year. His practice from the start was a criminal one. By the time of the prosecution of Thompson and Bywaters he had already made a considerable name by appearing in such famous cases as that of Oscar Wilde, Dr Hawley Harvey Crippen, George Joseph Smith of "The Brides in the Bath" and, later George John Haigh "The Acid Bath Murderer". In 1916 Humphrey's was appointed a senior Treasury Counsel which meant that his practice became one of prosecuting.

Prior to the Thompson-Bywaters trial he had successfully prosecuted Frederick Seddon, Sir Roger Casement and Horatio Bottomly. He was appointed a judge of the High Court in 1928. After the Second World War he sat with the Lord Chief Justice, Lord Goddard and Mr Justice Lynskey to hear the appeal of William Joyce against his conviction for treason. The appeal was dismissed. In 1950 Humphreys sat with Lord Goddard and Mr Justice Sellars to hear the appeal of Timothy Evans against his conviction for the murder of his infant daughter. This appeal was also dismissed.

Roland Oliver, third counsel for the Crown, was a distinguished advocate who ultimately became a High Court judge.

Leading Counsel for Bywaters was Cecil Whiteley KC. Whiteley was a competent and experienced barrister but his brief was a hopeless one. The prospect of persuading an unsympathetic jury that his client was acting in self-defence, or at least as an unthinking reaction to a move by Mr Thompson but with no intention to kill, was very poor indeed.

Leading for the defence of Thompson was Sir Henry Curtis-Bennett KC. Henry Honeywood Curtis-Bennett was the son of a Chief Metropolitan Magistrate. He was appointed King's Counsel in 1919 and received a knighthood in 1922 for his work in the secret service during the war years. He became the epitome of the "fashionable silk", a sobriquet which fitted him well since he was something of a showman. He appeared in many famous cases and was a great name, among others, who graced what has become known as the "Golden Age of the Bar".

Yet it may be questioned whether Curtis-Bennett was the best counsel for Mrs Thompson. It has been said that the great advocate Sir Edward Marshall Hall believed he could have won an acquittal for her. Would his forceful, dominating style have proved more effective than Sir Henry's gentle artistry? Would Curtis-Bennett have been wiser not to appeal to the emotions of the jury and to concentrate solely on the absence of evidence that Edith, though present, was not "aiding and abetting the murder of her husband?" Above all, could he have persuaded his client not to pursue the suicidal course of giving evidence? We shall never know.

Three Cases that Shook the Law

CHAPTER 4

The Indictment

The wording of the indictment upon which the case against the two defendants rested is of crucial importance. To lawyers that will be an obvious statement, but in this particular case it needs to be kept in mind from start to finish. This is because of the ancient principle in English courts of law that from first to last the burden of proof lies squarely upon the prosecution, and that proof must apply to every element in the indictment before an accused person can be convicted of being guilty. The graver the charge the more important the rule, because if that precept is breached the greater the injustice.

In the King against Frederick Edward Francis Bywaters and Edith Jessica Thompson there were two indictments. The first contained one offence only, the second contained five offences or counts.

The one offence charged in the first indictment was that Frederick Bywaters and Edith Thompson on the 4 day of October 1922 murdered Percy Thompson.

The second indictment contained the following: That Frederick Bywaters and Edith Thompson on the 20 day of August 1921 and on diverse dates between that date and the second day of October 1922 in the County of Essex and within the jurisdiction of the Central Criminal Court conspired together to murder Percy Thompson.

The remaining counts which concerned Edith alone were: soliciting to murder; inciting to commit a misdemeanour; administering poison with intent to murder; and administering a destructive thing with intent to murder. Those counts were not proceeded with, that is to say the Crown (prosecution) confined their case to the wording of the first indictment.

We therefore have to consider what it was that the Crown had to prove in order to obtain a conviction.

The ancient principle in English law has always been expressed with the Latin phrase *actus non facit nisi mens sit rea*. The deed does not make a person guilty unless his or her mind be guilty. Justice Stephen in *R v Tolson* (1889) defined this rule as follows:

> "The principle involved appears to me, when fully considered, to amount to no more than this. The full definition of every crime contains expressly or by implication a proposition as to a state of mind. Therefore if the mental element of any crime alleged to be a crime is proved to have been absent in any given case the crime as so defined is not committed, or again if a crime is fully defined nothing amounts to the crime which does not satisfy that definition."

Lord Reid, in the case *R v. Sweet and Parsley* (1970, Ac. p.132) said:

> "To make a man liable to imprisonment for an offence which he does not know that he is committing and is unable to prevent is repugnant to the ordinary man's conception of justice and brings the law into contempt."

Lord Reid laid down the following specific requirements as to the state of mind of the person charged. Firstly,

> "Foresight of the consequences by which it must be proved that the accused intended (in murder, death or really serious bodily injury) is no more than existence of the intent; it must be considered and its weight assessed together with all the evidence in the case. Foresight of consequences may be a fact from which the jury may think it right to infer the necessary intent. Secondly, where, exceptionally, it is insufficient to give the jury the simple direction that is for them to decide whether the defendant intended to kill or do serious bodily harm, they should be told that they are not entitled to find the necessary intention unless they feel sure that death or bodily harm was a virtual certainty barring some unforeseen intervention as a result of the defendant's actions and that the defendant appreciated that such was

the case. They should always be told that the decision is theirs to be made on a consideration of the whole of the evidence."

Thirdly "In appropriate cases it will be necessary to explain to the jury that intention is something quite different from motive or desire."

This principle of law was followed in a number of cases from 1985 to 1999. The leading case on the subject being the *R v. Moulin* (1999) (82 HL).

It is necessary to consider first principles and then apply these to the facts of the Thompson situation. Edith was charged with being a principal in the second degree in the murder of Percy. The Crown had to prove that she was present aiding and abetting his murder by Freddie Bywaters. It is not enough that she desired his death nor that she had the motive for the homicide. It had to be proved that at the moment of Bywaters stabbing Percy, Edith aided and abetted, that is to say assisted in and cooperated with Bywaters in his fatal action.

In the case of the *R v. Stringer* (2011) (Crim. App. Rep. 24 CA) the court held that "there may be cases where any assistance or encouragement proved is so distant in time place or circumstance from the conduct of the principal that it would be unjust to regard the principal's act as done with the defendant's encouragement or assistance but this is a matter for the for the jury. The key issue in the Thompson and Bywaters trial and the one upon which the defence should have concentrated, was were letters written by Edith months before the crime genuine appeals to Bywaters to murder or were they the fantasy outpouring of a woman's uncontrolled emotions?. The crucial question is was there evidence that Edith had planned the murder with her lover and fully cooperated in it's commission? It is submitted that such evidence as there is goes entirely to the contrary.

Mr Justice Shearman's summing-up is not above criticism in some respects, but it sets out accurately the point in question in his direction to the jury:

> "I now turn to the case of Mrs Thompson, a case which I have no doubt you will carefully and conscientiously consider being desirous of doing real

justice. Of course, if you should find that this was not a murder at all there is an end of the matter.

If there never was any intention by the man to do it, or if he never premeditated it in the sense that he only did it because he was provoked by a blow, if you believe the story that he was struck by a blow that so excited him that he did something that he had no thought of doing before, and did not come there to do in fact, it is manslaughter, not murder and there is an end of the matter, because the lady cannot be convicted of doing something which was done under provocation and never designed. If you think it is a murder then comes the question, is this lady a party to it?

Now, I am going to ask you to consider only one question in your deliberations, and that is was it an arranged thing between the woman and the man? I quite accept the law of the learned Solicitor-General that if you hire an assassin and say "Here is money, and there is a bargain between them that the assassin shall go out and murder the man when he can, the person who hires the assassin is guilty of the murder. It is plain common sense. I also accept the proposition that if a woman says to a man "I want this man murdered; you promise me to do it and he then promises her (She believing that he is going to keep his promise as soon as he gets an opportunity) and goes out and murders someone, then she also is guilty of murder. She is just as much guilty of murder if she lets loose an assassin as if she fires an arrow at a distance which pierces somebody's heart. But I do not think that is quiet the case that you have got to consider here.

At half past five, she leaves him telling him where she is going, and that she is coming back with her husband in the evening .If you think it was no surprise to her when she saw him that evening and if you think that when she saw him there that evening he came there under her direction, under her information that she would be there about that time, and that she had given him as to where she would be and that she was waiting there for their arrival under her direction and information that she had given him as to where she would be there about that time. If you think she knew perfectly well as soon as she set eyes on him he was there to murder, she is guilty of the murder too, because he was doing it under her direction with the hand that she was guiding. If you think that he had that knife in his pocket intending to murder of course this question only arises if you think he had that knife in his pocket intending to murder that evening and if you think she knew that he had it, I think it necessarily follows that, she would know that he was going to do it that evening.

That is what I submit to you. Therefore I think the only case I am going to ask you to consider is this: was she a party already to the murder in that sense, that she was aiding and abetting it? The words are pretty plain, aiding and abetting means giving a help to the murderer, if it actually took place."

The judge then went on to deal with the letters, but his direction to the jury on the definition of aiding and abetting cannot be faulted. Sir Montague Shearman had targeted the real issue in the case. The jury had to be satisfied beyond reasonable doubt that whatever may have been in the mind of Edith Thompson when she wrote the incriminating letters, when that murder took place on that date and time was she aiding and abetting its committal?. Beyond question there was such a doubt and that is why she was wrongly convicted and executed and why a posthumous pardon although never granted, is well merited.

In his work *The Innocence of Edith Thompson* Lewis Broad describes the atmosphere in number one court at the Old Bailey at the opening of the trial:

"The trial of Thompson and Bywaters was the five day wonder of its time. Like the advance publicity of a circus the police court proceedings had worked up a frenzy of public interest in the life and death drama to be staged in the Old Bailey. It was a spectacle with the minimum of accommodation for the public to secure the coveted seats in the gallery over number one court. Queues began to form at three o'clock in the morning, women, it was noted far outnumbered the men. Poison and passion, love, hate, murder, the youthful lover and the unfaithful wife. The fates had mixed ingredients with a generous hand for this Lyceum melodrama from actual life. There were long hours to wait but at last the doors were opened. The advance files of the queue were admitted, hundreds were turned away."

Sometimes in a murder trial, attempts are made to ensure an impartial jury by the system in which counsel may challenge those members who may, for one reason or another, have become influenced by what they have learnt about the case before hand.

In this particular trial the widespread publicity generated by the earlier proceedings in the Magistrates' Court would have ensured that members of the jury would be conversant with much of the detail, including the fact of the incriminating letters.

Before the jury were sworn in counsel for Bywaters, Cecil Whitely KC made an application to the judge for separate trials for each of the defendants. Where two defendants appear jointly on the same charge there may be a case for separating them.

This can occur when the evidence to be called against one of the defendants is prejudicial to the other. Again, if there are several charged jointly or with an offence which embraces the whole group, such as conspiracy, an individual who is on the periphery of the crime alleged may suffer from guilt by associating with the others, or whose contact with their activity is so tenuous that it may merit having his case dealt with separately.

However Mr Justice Shearman was peremptory: "I can see no reason for granting the application".

Sir Henry Curtis-Bennett then made a submission which was of vital importance to the case of Edith Thompson. He applied to have the evidence of the letters which she had written to Bywaters excluded. Had he succeeded in this there would have been no case against his client. Sir Henry set out the nub of his submission:

> "If there were some act committed by Mrs Thompson, the prosecution might then argue to your lordship that they were entitled to put these letters in evidence, either to show intent to rebut the defence of accident, or to show a system; but until some act, some definitive act, is proved by the prosecution as against Mrs Thompson, then I submit that all these letters

go to show is that if the letters really mean what they are said to mean, Mrs Thompson is a person who would not be likely to commit the offence which is charged against her."

"Is not this evidence of felonious intention of this lady, who it is alleged, was present at the murder?" Asked the judge.

Sir Henry replied:

"Not upon this indictment. It would be evidence, I agree, and I would not be able to object to these letters upon the second indictment. Supposing these letters really mean what upon the face of them they look to mean. This letter that I am referring you to (exhibit 18) was in fact written on 24th April of this year. Now the death of Mr Thompson took place in the early morning of 4th October of this year. Can it possibly be said that a letter written, even if it does mean what it looks to mean on the face of it, upon the 24th April of this year can be evidence, that upon 4th October, Mrs Thompson who certainly struck no blow, was a party to the killing of her husband six months after? There is surely a locus poenitentiae for everyone, and if a letter is written and is even meant to convey that Mrs Thompson was anxious in April that her husband should die, can it possibly be said to be evidence, that she, although present and not striking any blow upon 4th October, was in fact a party, a principal to the killing of her husband? I submit not."

After questions from the judge Sir Henry developed his argument further:

"If present she (Edith Thompson), would become a principal in the second degree. If not present and had taken some previous part in the matter, then she would be an accessory before the fact. It is really an academic question, the position of Mrs Thompson. But the fact remains that the prosecution desire to put this letter, and other letters of a similar sort, over dates which vary from November 1921 until August 1922, before the jury for the purpose not of showing that something that Mrs Thompson did constituted murder, but of proving, as they suggest, that she was guilty of murder. These letters in my submission are the only evidence of murder, if they were evidence against Mrs Thompson at all. The whole of the rest of the evidence relating to the night of the 3rd October and the early morning of the 4th October is absolutely consistent with Mrs Thompson having been taken by surprise in the attack which was made upon her husband, and knowing nothing about it at all. If the prosecution can show some act by Mrs Thompson which has to have some light thrown upon it to show whether or not it is an innocent act or a guilty act, then those letters might be admissible. But before they become admissible, they have got to show some such intent, and in my submission the writing of these letters months before October is too distant from the date of the alleged crime, and cannot be said to be evidence as to what Mrs Thompson was doing upon 3rd October."

The Solicitor-General rose to reply. The recently knighted Sir Thomas Inskip, who was to excel in both law and politics, was, like Mr Justice Shearman, a stern moralist. Like the judge we may have little reason to doubt that leading counsel for the Crown was as personally shocked by the whole drama before him. Both were religious men. The judge was a devout high churchman and Inskip was prominent in evangelical circles.

"As regards Mrs Thompson, I submit they [the letters] are admissible because she is being charged as a principal in the second degree, and they are admissible to show that she gave the incitement without which we say the murder would not have been committed, and that is the way in which she is brought into the case. She is indicted as the law permits, in the murder, although she did not strike the blow. The crime is one where one hand struck the blow, and we want to show by these letters that her mind conceived it and incited it, the evidence of that is in the letters that Mrs Thompson wrote to the man who struck the blow.

The case of the *King v Armstrong* is, as your lordship said, a very different case indeed. There was a question as to whether letters or evidence which showed a crime against B had been contemplated was in any way evidence against A and it was said that a certain foundation ought to be laid before you could bring evidence of the other matters. That is not the case here.

Those letters are evidence of the particular crime which is charged, namely that she prompted the crime and incited a crime, and she is therefore a principal in the second degree. As against Bywaters the letters are found in his possession, they are evidence of motive."

Once again Mr Justice Shearman, with his usual brevity, declared in favour of admitting the letters in evidence.

"I think these letters, letters such as the ones to which Sir Henry Curtis-Bennett referred, are admissible as evidence of intention and of motive, and I shall admit them. Objections can be taken in the proper way when they come up. Only one other matter. I do not think you can contest the letters showing the affectionate relations between the parties are not evidence of motive in so far as they show affection."

Three Cases that Shook the Law

CHAPTER 5

The Opening Speech of the Solicitor-General

The Solicitor-General rose to make the opening statement for the Crown. Whatever criticism may be made of his address to the jury it can never be said that Sir Thomas Inskip was not an honourable man and a respected figure in both the legal and political world, nor should he be censured for making telling points for the Crown whose case it was his duty to prosecute. However there are grounds for thinking that some points in his speech were simplistic and partial. His introductory words to the jury, which consisted of eleven men and one woman, although the judge referred to them as "gentlemen" rather than as members of the jury, were as follows:

> "May it please your Lordship, members of the jury — on 4th October, a little after midnight, Percy Thompson was stabbed to death on his way home from Ilford station, near which he lived. He was in a dark part of a road not over well-lit at the best of times, when he was struck, first apparently from behind and then in front by some assailant. The only other person present was his wife, Mrs Thompson, who is now in the dock. She is charged with Bywaters, who is said by the prosecution to have been the assailant, in the murder of Percy Thompson. You will be able to distinguish as to the relevancy of the evidence as between Bywaters and Mrs Thompson. I give you that warning, before I come to the facts, in that you may the more closely, if possible, follow the evidence which I shall open, and which shall be given. I ask you to dismiss from your minds any suggestions you may have heard about this case in other places."

Two comments are appropriate at this stage. The first is that the place where the murders took place was neither unusually dark nor concealed. The corner area of Endsleigh Gardens and Belgrave Road was no better or worse lit than much of Ilford. That is made plain by the fact that there were people in the vicinity even at that hour immediately after the assault. However the description of the sight of the crime by the prosecution gives the clear impression that Edith and Frederick had planned the killing to take place at that particular spot. There is not a jot of evidence to support that suggestion.

The second comment relates to the jury. Very properly Inskip warned the jury that they must dismiss from their minds anything which they had read or heard about the case or which had been the subject of discussion they may have conducted with other people. It is usual and proper for the judge to apply a similar caution. But this can be a very optimistic exercise.

Sometimes efforts can be made to obtain a jury whose members are from an area well outside a district where the crime was committed, thus minimising the likelihood of their having been influenced in their views, hence their judgement, in trying the case before them. But this is not always possible. There was no chance at all that such a certainty of prejudice could be avoided in the trial of Thompson and Bywaters. The proceedings at the magistrates' court had received great publicity in the press and on radio. It was at that early stage already a *cause célèbre*. The contents of the letters would have become widely known, and in a society which viewed marital infidelity with greater severity than today a firm opinion of Edith and her lover would have been formed by a great many people.

The Solicitor-General then described the background, history and the development of the illicit affair between the two defendants, and then he turned to the letters. It is not surprising that these formed the bulk of his speech. The Crown lawyers knew full well that their difficulty might arise from the fact that at the moment of the murder Edith had shown shock and surprise which more than one witness at the scene was convinced was genuine. This ran completely contrary to the theory of a planned enterprise to which the prosecutor had nailed his colours. That

The Opening Speech of the Solicitor-General

is why Sir Thomas Inskip made careful provision for the contingency that the theory of a planned association might fail:

> "I suggest to you members of the jury that you will have to consider whether the hand that struck the blow was moved, was incited, to the crime by Mrs Thompson. It may be that the passion of the young man may have led him in that direction. It is no answer that the whole of the incitement should come from Mrs Thompson. There is the undoubted evidence in the letters upon which you can find that there was a preconcerted meeting between Mrs Thompson and Bywaters. At the place. But supposing you were not fully satisfied that there was a conspiracy made to effect the murder at this place and time, if you are satisfied that Mrs Thompson incited the murder and that, incited and directed by her controlling hand, Bywaters committed the murder then it will be my duty to ask you after hearing the evidence, to find her who incited and proposed the murder as guilty as Bywaters who committed it."

There is in fact no undoubted "evidence" in the letters upon which the jury could find that there was a preconceived meeting between Thompson and Bywaters at the place of the murder.

Now let us turn to the letters. These fall into three categories. These are, firstly, those which simply contain passionate expressions of love and desire; secondly those which embody words which can be construed as malign feelings towards her husband to the extent that Edith wishes him harm of one kind or another; and thirdly those which, whether serious or foolish fantasising to please her lover, are unmissable signs that Edith would have been very happy to see her husband dead.

The prosecution placed before the jury the six letters in the second two groups. The others were not read to them. The first letter to give an indication of Edith's feeling of animosity towards Percy is that on the 10th February 1922:

> "Darlint you must do something this time—I am not really impatient—but opportunities come and go by—they have to—because I am helpless and I think and think and think—perhaps it will never come again."

63

A later passage says: "It would be so easy darlint — if I had things — I do hope I shall." This and other letters were accompanied by newspaper cuttings containing reports of poisoning and attempts to poison.

It is clear that throughout his speech Inskip is hedging his bets. On the one hand he claims that Edith was inciting Bywaters to murder her husband, but he was fair enough to agree that the incitement must continue to the murder itself to make her guilty. On the other hand he maintains that the letters after the 23rd September, coupled with her actions, show that she was party to a conspiracy to murder Percy, in co-operation with Bywaters, at the place and time when his death occurred. In fact both the tenor of her letters and her words and actions on the 3rd October provide an answer to both allegations. They show that the incitement, if such there was, did not exist at the time of the murder, and make it plain that Bywaters was acting independently.

The letters in the third category which are the most prejudicial to the defence are those of April and May which refer to broken glass and knowledge of poisons. What was noticeably absent from the speech of the Solicitor-General, but which became plain as the trial proceeded was, firstly the patent absurdity of the glass allegations, the absence of any evidence that Edith had attempted at any time to obtain poison and the all-important testimony of Sir Bernard Spilsbury that no trace of either glass or poison was found in the body of Thompson at the autopsy.

What is very clear from the letters in September and onwards is that they indicate a cooling in the relationship of Freddie and Edith. From the tone of her replies there can be no doubt that the peripatetic Freddie was looking for a way out of a situation which, in spite of the expressions of ardour by both parties, was going nowhere. The letter Exhibit 28 written by Edith after the 19th September makes this apparent. It is worth considering at length:

> "I think I'm fearfully disappointed about you not getting in on Friday darlint. I'd been planning to get off early — rush to Ilford, and do the shopping and rush up to meet you, having had my hair washed in the lunch hour instead of at night — as I should have, and now all that is no use — so I shan't have my hair washed — it must wait until next Friday — that will

mean an extra hour with you — do you mind me having a dirty head for a week darlint, its very very dirty. I've been hanging it out just for now. Why are you so late this time — oh I hate this journey, I hate Australia and everything connected with it — it will be 109 days since I've seen you — and you didn't answer my question about China and Japan next time. I suppose it is right or you would have told me — it will be worse then.

I was surprised at you going home this time darlint — so surprised that I couldn't believe that I had read rightly at first.

You ask me if I am glad or sorry darlint, I don't know how I feel about it. I am pleased for you darlint — because you know I always felt responsible for the break. I don't think I'm glad for myself though. I think I'm harbouring just a small petty feeling of resentment against them. I've tried so hard not to — and I think I didn't at first, and its only just this last time.

You say you have reasons darlint, I don't know them and you don't tell me them, so I can't be influenced by them one way or the other. Tell me them — it will help darlingest. You say you suppose you deserve the Sydney letter, didn't you get two darlint, I was very sorry as soon as I had posted the first — I do hope you get the second.

Darlint boy — pal — you are horrid to be cross about the Turkish delight — you are really — I'm sorry I wrote that — but just think darlint — you know that is what everyone else would have said or thought and I'm mixed up with all the "everyones" so much that I forgot at the moment that I was talking to someone different. If you are still cross soften a wee tiny bit and forgive Piedi and try and accept her excuse for everything darlint — you know 'to err is human — to forgive divine' and I am certainly not going to even hazard a guess why you are not bringing any delight or cigarettes this time, in case I err again or am misunderstood. Please tell me. I think I must have been reading 'The Firing Line' at the same time as you — I finished it last Sunday. Why didn't you like it as well as the others darlint?"

There follows some discussion regarding books then comes this very significant passage:

"Darlingest boy—I don't quite understand you about pals; you say can we be pals only, Piedi, it will make is easier. Do you mean for always because if you do, no, no, a thousand times. We can't be pals only for always darlint—it's impossible physically and mentally.

Last time we had a long talk—I said go away this time and forget all about me, forget that you ever knew me, it will be easier—and better for you. Do you remember—and you refused, so now I am refusing darlint—it must be still the hope of all or the finish of all. If you still only mean for a certain time and you think it's best, darlint it shall be so—I don't see how it will be easier myself—but it shall be as you say and wish we won't be our natural selves. I know tho—we'll be putting a curb on ourselves the whole time—like an iron hand that won't expand. Please don't let what I have written deter you from my decision darlint, I don't want to do that—truly I'd like to do what you think best."

The letter continues to deal with Edith's health and the addressing of letters to Freddie. Then:

"Now about that Wednesday I mentioned—I am disappointed. I thought you told me you'd never forget 'don't spoil it' and yet you can remember a trivial incident like that. Monday when I was with Harry Penton do you remember now? Taking me to a quick lunch at Evans and coming into 168 and then meeting your mother up west and then ringing me and asking me what I was doing that evening—and I was going to tea at the Warldorf. You went and slept at Norwood that night and didn't come back to me until Friday. You sound very despondent when you say about 'time passes and with it some of the pain—fate ordained our lot to be hard'. Does some of the pain you feel pass with time? Perhaps it does—things seem so much easier to forget with a man—his environment is always different—but with a woman it is always the same. Darlint my pain gets less and less bearable, it hurts more and more every day, every hour really.

The Opening Speech of the Solicitor-General

Other ways only involve the parting of you and I, Peidi, nobody deserves anything more than I do.

I don't understand this part—try and explain to me please, have you lost heart and given up hope? Tell me if you have darlint—don't bear it all alone. "Darlingest, about you being unnatural—I don't know—I don't think it's unnatural to give something without wanting to receive in return—I never did—but I think at one time—you would have thought so.

From the way your acquaintances argue—they are judging you from how they know you, I think, but I know quite a different boy from them.—He's a pal—not an ordinary sensual sort of creature made in the usual mould of men.

Let them know you as they like darlint, I'm selfish enough to be the only one who really knows her pal. I think I must be fearfully dense—also my memory has left me in the lurch—because I don't understand what you mean by your question "Peidi, do you think you could live with a replica?—you once said no! When did I say it, and what do you mean—what does the question refer to? It's a puzzle to me darlint, but I accept the rebuff my memory has given me and hope you will overlook this omission.

Darlint, that's the worst of saying something 'is always good' it invariably lets you down after this statement, please explain.

Now I am going to be cross—don't bully me—I never said or even suggested that I should cultivate the Regent Park Hotel and there was no need whatever for you to have hurled forth that edict and then underlined it. Ask to be forgiven—you bully! (darlint pal)."

The remainder of the passage concerns a watch, but includes the words: "Yes darlint, you are jealous of him—but I want you to be—he has the right by law to all that you have the right to by nature and love—yes darlint, be jealous, so much that you will do something desperate."

This letter which was referred to so briefly by Sir Thomas Inskip in his opening address is of great importance since it shows without any question of doubt that the affair of the two lovers was running into trouble. Bywaters is looking for a way out. He is starting to stay with his mother rather than the Graydons when he is on shore—greatly to Edith's surprise and resentment. More significantly, he wants them to be "pals". He is clearly anxious to reduce the torrid affair to a mere friendship. At this suggestion Edith shows signs of panic. She, notwithstanding her professed adoration of the young Adonis, has told him, "go away this time and forget all about me, forget you ever knew me, it will be easier—and better for you." "Do you remember—and you refused, so now I am refusing darlint—it must be still 'the hope of all or the finish of all'." Here is Edith going so far as to suggest ending their relationship? Comparatively minor issues begin to rankle. "Now about that Wednesday I mentioned—I am disappointed. I thought you told me you'd never forget. Don't spoil it. And yet you can remember a trivial incident like that."

Edith is all too conscious of Freddie's change of heart: "I don't understand this part—try and explain to me please—have you lost heart and given up hope? Tell me if you have darlint—don't bear it all alone".

Again more significantly: "I think I must be fearfully dense, also my memory has left me in the lurch because I don't understand what you mean by your question 'Peidi, do you think you could live with a replica?'—You once said 'no'. Is Bywaters testing Edith's reaction to his departure and the arrival of another in his place?

Perhaps most pointed of all: "Now I am going to be cross—don't bully me, I never said or even suggested that I should cultivate the Regent Palace Hotel and there was no need whatsoever for you to have hurled that edict and then underlined it. Ask to be forgiven you bully? (darlint pal)". The obvious reference to be drawn from these passages is surely that with the affair fading Edith was in no mind to co-operate with Bywaters in the terrible crime of murder, least of all the murder of her husband.

In dealing with the letters what is apparent is the fact that the Solicitor-General quotes those passages which he maintains support the prosecution case but omits those which are favourable to the accused.

The Opening Speech of the Solicitor-General

Nowhere is this more evident than the manner in which he puts his own slant on the letter Exhibit 60 written just before the day of the murder:

> "Darlingest lover of mine thank you, thank you oh thank you a thousand times for Friday, it was lovely it's always lovely to go to go out with you.
>
> And then Saturday yes I did feel happy, I didn't think a teeny bit about anything in this world, except being with you — and all Saturday evening I was thinking about you I was just with you in a big arm chair in front of a big fire all the time thinking how much I had won — 'cos I have darlint, won such a lot it feels such a great big thing to me sometimes that I can't breathe.
>
> When you are away and I see girls with men walking along together- perhaps they are acknowledged sweethearts — they look so ordinary then I feel proud to think that you are my lover and although not acknowledged I can still hold you — just with a tiny 'hope'.
>
> Darlint, we said we'll always be pals haven't we, shall we say we will always be lovers even 'tho secret ones, or is it (this great big love) a thing we can't control — dare we say that — I think I will dare. Yes, I will always love you, if you are dead — if you have left me even if you don't still love me, I always shall you. Your love to me is new, it is something different, it is my life and if things should go badly with us I shall always have this past year to look upon and feel that 'then I lived'. I never did before and never shall again.
>
> Darlingst lover, what happened last night? I don't know myself. I only know how I felt — no not really how I felt but how I could feel — if time and circumstances were different.
>
> It seems like a great welling up of love, of feeling inertia, just as if I am wax in your hands — to do with as you will and I feel if you do as you wish I shall be happy. Its physical purely and I can't really describe it — but you will understand darlint won't you? You said you knew it would be like this someday — If it hadn't would you have been disappointed?. Darlingst when you are rough I go dead — try not to be please.

> The book is lovely-it's going to be sad darlint tho', why can't life go on happy always. I like Clarie, she is so natural, so unworldly. Why aren't you an artist and I as she is—I feel when I am reading frightfully jealous of her—It's a picture darlint, just how I did once picture that little flat in Chelsea—why can't he go on loving her always—why are men different—I am right when I say that love to a man is a thing apart from his life but to a woman it is her whole existence."

Edith spoke of the consequences if her husband knew she was going to meet Bywaters:

> "There would be scenes and he would come to 168 and interfere and I couldn't bear that. I could be beaten all over at home and still be defiant—but at 168 its different, it's my living—you wouldn't let me live on him would you and you and I shouldn't want to. Darlint its funds that is our stumbling block—until we have these we can do nothing. Darlint find me a job abroad. I'll go tomorrow and not say I was going to a soul and not have one little regret. I said I wouldn't think that, I'd try to forget circumstances pal, help me forget again I have succeeded up to now but its thinking of tonight and tomorrow when I can't see you and feel you are holding me.
>
> Darlint—do something tomorrow night will you? Something to make you forget. I'll be hurt I know, but I want you to hurt me, I do really—the bargain now seems so one sided—so unfair but how can I alter it?"

There then follows a passage regarding a watch. Then these words:

> "He's still well—he's he is going to gaze all day long at you in your temporary home after Wednesday.
>
> Don't forget what we talked about in the Tea Room, I'll still risk and try if you will—we only have 3 and ¾ years left darlingst. Try and help."

Referring to that ultimate passage Inskip says:

The Opening Speech of the Solicitor-General

"That is a rather cryptic reference to a period that Mrs Thompson mentions more than once. She speaks sometimes of four years then fifteen months have passed and now she says there are three and ¾ years left. I ask—what did they talk about in the Tea Room? I put it that there was a long course of suggestion resulting in a desire to escape from the position, and a fresh suggestion was made in the Tea Room."

This assertion by Sir Thomas is wholly unfounded and unwarranted. He knows full well that there is no evidence whatsoever regarding that conversation between Edith and Frederick. He does not say that murder was planned so he makes an unjust inference that this was the subject discussed. That suggestion emerged from the prosecutor's own imagination only. It is wrong, and borders on the improper.

In his closing speech for Edith Thompson, Sir Henry Curtis Bennet makes a telling response:

"The next passage in the letter is 'don't forget about what we talked about in the Tea Room, I'll still risk and try if you will'.

The suggestion of the prosecution—and they have no evidence at all of it—is that in the Tea Room in Aldergate Street these two people were plotting murder. There is not a scrap of evidence. But having put all those letters before you and having created the prejudice those letters must create when first read without an explanation, the prosecution then say 'the night of the 3rd October Thompson dies and don't forget what was talked about in the Tea Room'—and you members of the jury are urged to believe that they were talking about murder. Both the prisoners have been in the witness box and have told you how the conversation was the same story as to taking Mrs Thompson away, as to her leaving her husband and risking all her future with Bywaters. Is it not shown that is the way to look at the sentence when the last words of the letter read 'we only have three and three quarters years left, darlingest try and help Peidi?' It is almost inconceivable that it can be suggested on that letter, or to think that seriously the prosecution can say that it shows that these two people were plotting murder. The words show quite the contrary; do you imagine that a woman who at that time, according to the prosecution, had got to the degree of having incited this man to the extent that the murder is imminent, would be writing we have only three and three quarter years left. If the story put before you by the prosecution be true do you not think you would find in these letters some references egging on, inciting, soliciting Bywaters to commit this murder? Yet you find in my submission, exactly the opposite. There is not one reference in these letters which anyone in this country dare say shows that the suggestion made by the prosecution is true."

The Solicitor-General concluded by referring to the voice of Edith Thomson being heard to call out, "Oh my god, will you help me? My husband is 'dying'?" He made no mention of her voice being heard to call "Oh don't, oh don't." Speaking of the occasion when Edith saw Bywaters at the Ilford Police Station it was said she was very agitated and exclaimed "My god, what can I do? Why did he do it? I did not want him to do it. I must tell the truth. I saw my husband struggling with Freddie Bywaters."

Now let us turn to the evidence.

CHAPTER 6

The Evidence for the Prosecution

Mr Justice Shearman, in that part of his charge to the jury which concerned Edith Thompson, put the case against her in a single sentence: "Now, I am going to ask you to consider only one question in your deliberations, and that is was it an arranged thing between the woman and the man?"

It follows from that direction that if the answer to the question was "Yes" then Edith was guilty as charged. If the answer was "No" she should be acquitted. If the jury had disagreed with the Solicitor-General when he said, "There is undoubted evidence in the letters upon which you can find that there was a pre-concerted meeting between Mrs Thompson and Bywaters at the place," then Edith would, and in this author's submission should, have left the Old Bailey a free woman.

Sir Thomas Inskip however was clearly aware of the dearth of evidence of a conspiracy between Edith and Freddie in the Tea Room. He therefore "hedged his bets" by introducing as an alternative theory the allegation of enticement:

> "But supposing you were not wholly satisfied that there was a conspiracy made to effect the murder at this place and time, if you are satisfied that Mrs Thompson incited the murder and that, incited and directed by her controlling hand Bywaters committed the murder, then it will be my duty to ask you, after hearing the evidence, to find her who incited and proposed the murder as guilty as Bywaters who committed it."

It is always the duty of the prosecution to make it plain how the case is "put".

At the commencement of his address to the jury, Sir Henry Curtis-Bennett was clearly concerned to understand exactly how the case was presented against his client:

> "For some reason — you, members of the jury, may possibly understand the reason; I don't pretend to — the prosecution have here elected to put these two people in the dock together and charge them with murder. As far as I know there is no other case in which a jury have been empanelled to try either man or woman with murder where it could not be alleged by the prosecution that that person did any act when the murder, if it was murder, was committed. By the prosecution it is stated that Mrs Thompson was what is known as the principal in the second degree, namely a person who 'aids, abets or assists a murderer when he is committing a murder.'"

Mr Justice Shearman: That is not exclusive. If two people contrive to murder they are guilty of murder even if one was not there.
Sir Henry Curtis-Bennett: Yes he is an accessory.
Mr Justice Shearman: You say he is not guilty of murder, if he did not actually take part in it?
Curtis-Bennett: I am not going to shirk any issue. It is no good when representing somebody to try and put before the jury some story which does not meet the case at all. It cannot be alleged that anything further might be charged against her.
Mr Justice Shearman: Of course a person might be regarded as an accessory before the fact.
Curtis-Bennett: If the case as suggested by the prosecution were that Mrs Thompson knew what was going to happen that night, and that she took the person who was to be murdered to the spot where he was murdered, then I would welcome that case. The jury would see that the whole of the evidence was to the contrary in such a case.

Sir Henry continued to the jury, having assisted the judge in his understanding of the law:

"If you come to the conclusion that she conspired with Bywaters to murder her husband on that night, then you will convict her on that indictment if you come to the conclusion that she was urging Bywaters on. At this moment however she sits in the dock charged with being a murderess on the night of the 3rd October and it is for the prosecution to satisfy you that she is guilty. I suppose that the case for the prosecution is founded upon nothing but those letters written over a period of time, and founded outside that, on nothing but guesswork, contradicted when you come to test it. I suppose the case is that there was an arrangement on that night that Thompson should be murdered, that Mrs Thompson was a party to it, and that Mrs Thompson knew quite well as she was walking down the road near her home that at any moment her husband was going to be taken from her side and murdered in cold blood. I contend that every single action of Mrs Thompson upon the night when the killing took place shows that she knew nothing of what was going to happen."

Let us consider what those actions were. Criticisms may be made of the judge and of counsel for the Crown. These may be valid, but they are largely peripheral to the main issue. That is: was there sufficient evidence to convict Edith of the offence charged or does such evidence fall short of that requirement?

John Laxton, an uncle of Percy Thompson, said:

"From time to time I met him [Percy] and his wife, the prisoner Thompson. On Tuesday 3rd October, I met them both by arrangement at the Criterion Theatre; I think the arrangement was made by my wife about a week or a fortnight beforehand. After the performance was over we left Mr and Mrs Thompson at the Piccadilly tube station, about quarter to eleven or eleven o'clock. They were going to Liverpool Street, and went down a different lift to what we did."

Cross-examined by Sir Henry Curtis-Bennett:

"I had gone on several occasions before to the theatre with Mr and Mrs Thompson. So far as I could see they appeared to be on good terms. The party on the particular evening to which I have spoken was an ordinary happy theatre party, and when Mr and Mrs Thompson left us at the tube station they appeared to be on their usual terms."

Dora Pittard gave important evidence as to the condition of Edith:

"I live at 59 Endsleigh Gardens, Ilford. A few minutes before midnight on the 3rd October I arrived with some friends of mine at Ilford station, and I proceeded to walk home by Belgrave Road. When I was between De Vere Gardens and Endsleigh Gardens I saw a woman running towards me — the prisoner Mrs Thompson. She cried out, 'Oh my God! Will you help me; my husband is ill, he is bleeding.' I asked her where he was and she said he was on the pavement. I took Mrs Thomson to the house of Dr Maudsley, at the corner of Courtland Avenue, and I then went back to Kensington Gardens, Mrs Thompson being just in front of me. Finding a man lying on the pavement I asked Mrs Thompson what had happened to her husband, and she said, 'Oh don't ask me, I don't know. Somebody flew past and when I turned to speak to him blood was pouring out of his mouth.' Mrs Thompson was very agitated and incoherent."

Dora Pittard: When I first saw Mrs Thompson she was running hard in my direction.
Sir Henry Curtis-Bennett: It was quite clear to you that at that time she was in a hysterical condition?
Pittard: Yes she was very agitated.
Curtis-Bennett: It was quite obvious to you that she wanted to get help for her husband?
Pittard: Yes, I suppose so.

Edith knew that the assailant was Bywaters but she foolishly sought to protect his identity. Percy Edward Clevely was one of the group who encountered Edith at the scene. He said:

"While walking through Belgrave Road we met the prisoner Mrs Thompson, who seemed to call out of the darkness, as it were. She spoke

The Evidence for the Prosecution

about her husband having fallen down, that he was ill, and she wanted help, and she asked where we could find a doctor. We went to Dr Maudsley's house, and on returning we found the deceased lying on the pavement with his back propped against the wall. I asked Mrs Thompson how it happened, and she said she could not say—'something brushed past'—or 'flew past' or words to that effect and he fell down."

Curtis-Bennett: When Mrs Thompson first came up 'Do you know a doctor, do you know a doctor' was not the first thing she said?
Percy Edward Clevely: No I think that the first thing was that she asked for help. She asked for a doctor and said that her husband had fallen down. On the way back to Dr Maudsley's Mrs Thompson ran in front of us to get back to her husband. When we got there we found her kneeling down with him.
Curtis-Bennett: When you asked her what had happened was she in a very agitated condition?
Clevely: Yes, she was certainly very excited and agitated.
Curtis-Bennett: And hysterical and incoherent in her statements?
Clevely: Yes.

Then came the evidence of John Webber, which the judge in his summing-up described as "curious". A better description would have been "crucial", because if accepted it nullifies the central part of the Crown case that the murder of Thompson was an arranged affair between Edith and Bywaters. The fact that Mr Justice Shearman made every effort to blunt its effectiveness is indicative of a grave lack of impartiality.

John Webber said that he was a sales manager and lived at 59 De Vere Gardens Ilford:

"About 12.30 in the morning of the 4th October, just as I was about to retire to bed I heard a woman's voice saying, "Oh don't, oh don't" in a most piteous manner. On hearing that I went out into the street, and I saw two ladies and a gentleman coming towards me in the direction of Dr Maudsley's house. One of the ladies was running in front of the other two. After they had passed me I saw a match being struck, and I went up to the place and found a man sitting against the wall. Mrs Thompson was there alone with him and I asked her if the man had had a fall, but she said she did not know. I asked her if I could be of any assistance to him and she said 'Don't touch him, don't touch him, a lady and gentleman have gone off for a doctor'. After that Dr Maudsley came with Miss Pittard and Mr Clevely. I helped the doctor to undress the man. I heard the doctor ask Mrs Thompson if he had been ill, and where they had come from. She told him that he had not been ill, and that they had come from the Criterion Theatre."

John Webber: I have no doubt whatever that the voice I heard 'oh don't, oh don't' was the voice of Mrs Thompson. It was about three or five minutes afterwards that I saw the three persons coming towards me. Mrs Thompson who was in the front, was sobbing and running hard. When I went across to where Mr Thompson was sitting on the pavement I found Mrs Thompson there evidently waiting for assistance. I asked her if he had a fall, and she said 'Yes—no—I don't know.'

Curtis-Bennett: It was quite evident was it not, that she was in a very agitated state at that time?

Webber: I should say she was almost hysterical.

Two things are apparent from the behaviour of Edith Thompson immediately after the murder. They are, firstly that she was in an agitated, distraught and almost hysterical condition. The second, that she did not for a while give a truthful account of what had happened.

Dr Maudsley, an experienced doctor well-practised in dealing with people in extreme situations resulting from illness or accident described Edith's condition as "confused", "hysterical" and "agitated". He said in his testimony: "When I told her that her husband was dead she said 'Why did you not come sooner and save him?'"

What are we to make of the evidence of the witnesses? They are intelligent and observant people who had every opportunity of studying the reactions and emotions of Edith at that fraught moment. Was she putting on an act? Could she possibly be in that condition if the murder was a jointly arranged action? Here was a woman running sobbing, hysterical, almost incoherent. Could this possibly be the outcome of a carefully arranged assassination? Perhaps the most significant indication can be found in the words of Detective Inspector Wensley, who played a major role in the investigation, contained in his book *Detective Days* written years later: "There was no doubt that her distress was genuine."

The whole scenario was completely inconsistent with a planned killing. Would the woman who allegedly incited Bywaters to use poison have agreed to such a barbaric attack with a knife?

The reason for Edith's failure to give a completely true picture of the crime is surely obvious. She was protecting Bywaters, her lover. This was undermining her chance of acquittal because it called into question her veracity. The prosecution were able to say if she cannot be believed regarding her explanation of the events at the time when they occurred what value can be placed in her denial of involvement?

Police Sergeant Walter Grimes went to Edith and Percy's house at 3 am on the 4th October:

> "I asked her if she could explain to me what had happened on the road home from the station. She said I don't know, I can't say, I only know that my husband suddenly dropped down and screamed out, oh. I then rushed across the road and saw a lady and a gentleman, and asked them if they would help me and they went with me to the doctor."

In answer to Sir Henry Curtis-Bennett, Sergeant Grimes said: "At that time she appeared to be very distressed and inclined to be hysterical."

Sgt Walter Anew went to Belgrave Road shortly after 1 am on the 4th October:

> "Mrs Thompson was there beside the body of her husband. After the body was removed by some other officers I went with her to her home 41 Kensington Gardens, which was quite close by. On the way there she said 'Will he come back?' and I replied 'Yes'. She then said 'they will blame me for this.' At three o'clock on that same morning I returned to 41 Kensington Gardens and saw Mrs Thompson again. I asked her 'Can you account for the cuts on your husband's neck? She replied 'No, we were walking along and my husband said "oh", I said "bear up" thinking he had one of his attacks.

He then fell on me and walked a little further. He then fell up against the wall and then onto the ground. I asked her 'Did he have a knife?' and she replied 'No I did not see a knife or anything.' I noticed that her coat and clothes and face had signs of blood on them, which would be natural if she had been holding up her husband or anybody else who was bleeding."

Detective Inspector Richard Sellars was the first police officer to whom Edith gave a fuller account of Percy's death:

"I said to her I am an inspector of police. I understand you were with your husband early this morning at Belgrave Road. I am satisfied that he was assaulted and stabbed several times.

She said 'We were coming along Belgrave Road, and just passed the corner of Endsleigh Gardens when I heard him call out "oh, er" and he fell up against me. I put out my arms to save him, and found blood, which I thought was coming from his mouth. I tried to help him. He staggered several yards towards Kensington Gardens, and then fell against the wall and slid down. He did not speak to me. I cannot say if I spoke to him. I felt him and found his clothing was wet with blood. He never moved after he fell. We had no quarrel on the way, we were quite happy together. Immediately I saw blood I ran across the road to a doctor's. I appealed to a lady and gentleman who were passing and the gentleman also went to the doctor's. The doctor came and told me my husband was dead.'

'Just before he fell down I was walking on his right hand side, on the inside pavement nearest the wall. We were side by side. I did not see anybody about at that time. My husband and I were talking about going to a dance.' At that time Mrs Thompson was in an agitated condition."

Detective Inspector Sellars took Edith to Ilford Police Station. She then made a full statement which was type written and signed by her:

"My husband's name is Percy Thompson. He is a shipping clerk employed by Messrs O J Parker and Co, Peel House, Eastcheap E C. I am employed

The Evidence for the Prosecution

by Carlton & Prior, millinery manufactures 168 Aldergate Street EC as a book-keeper. We have been married six years and have no family. We were married in the beginning of the year 1916. In that year my husband joined the London Scottish regiment, he was discharged as medically unfit a few months later and did no foreign service, I have always been on affectionate terms with my husband. I remember Tuesday 3rd October 1922. We both went to our respective businesses that day. I met my husband by appointment at a quarter to six in Aldersgate Street, that day we went to the Criterion Theatre, we were there met by my uncle and aunt Mr and Mrs J Laxton, we left the theatre about 11 pm, we all four went to the Piccadilly tube, we there separated, my husband and I went to Liverpool Street, and we caught the 11.30 train to Ilford. We arrived at Ilford about 12 o'clock, we then proceeded along York Road, Belgrave Road and when we got between De Vere and Endsleigh Gardens, (we were walking on the right hand side) my husband suddenly went into the roadway, I went after him, and he fell up against me, and called out 'ooer'. He was staggering, he was bleeding and I thought the blood was coming from his mouth, I cannot remember whether I saw anyone else there or not. I know there was no one there when he was staggering up against me. I got hold of my husband with both hands and assisted him to sit up against the wall. He stood there for about a minute or two and then slid down onto the footway, he never spoke. I fell to the ground with him. I cannot remember if I shouted out or not. I got up off the ground and ran along to Courtfield Avenue with the intention of calling Dr Maudsley, but on the way I met a lady and a gentleman and I said to them something to this effect 'Can I get a doctor to help me, my husband is ill.' The gentleman said 'I will go for the doctor.' Dr Maudsley arrived shortly after, although it seemed a long time. The doctor examined my husband and said that he was dead. An ambulance was sent for and the body was removed. I was accompanied to my home by two police officers.

I know Freddie Bywaters I have known him for several years; we were at school together, at least I wasn't but my two brothers were. He is residing with his widowed mother at 11 Westow Street, Norwood. He is a ship's writer and periodically goes away to sea. He has been for a very long time on visiting terms with my family. In June 1921 Bywaters came to reside with my husband and myself at Number 41 Kensington Gardens. He came as a paying guest. I think he paid twenty five shillings or twenty seven and sixpence per week. He was with us to the beginning of August 1921. My husband and I quarrelled about something, he struck me. I knocked a chair over, Freddie came in and interfered on my behalf. I left the room and I do not know what transpired between them. As far as my recollection goes Freddie left on the following Friday, but before he left my husband and he were friends again. We have been in the habit of corresponding with one another. His letters to me and mine to him were couched in affectionate terms. I am not in possession of any letters he writes to me. I have destroyed all as is customary with me with my correspondence. The letters shown to me by Inspector Hall and addressed to F Bywaters are some of the letters that I wrote to Freddie, and were written to him without my husband's consent. When he was at home in England, we were in the habit of going out occasionally together without my husband's knowledge." [Signed].

Then a dramatic incident intervened which completely altered the picture, Mr Sellars continued:

"After making that statement Mrs Thompson and I left the room; I took her to the matron's room. In doing so we passed the library, where Bywaters was detained. She saw him as she passed and said 'Oh lord, oh God, what can I do? Why did he do it? I did not want him to do it.' She further said almost immediately after: 'I must tell the truth.' She was a little hysterical, and I said: 'You realise what you are saying, what you might say may be used in evidence'. She then proceeded to make a statement, which again was written down and signed."

That statement was as follows:

"When we got near Endsleigh Gardens a man rushed out from the gardens and pushed me away from my husband. I was dazed for a moment. When I recovered I saw my husband scuffling with a man. The man whom I know as Freddie Bywaters was running away. He was wearing a blue overcoat and a grey hat. I know it was him although I did not see his face."

The Evidence for the Prosecution

After initially denying all knowledge of the murder Bywaters also agreed to make a statement:

"I have known Mr Percy Thompson for about four years and his wife Edith, for about seven years. Mr Thompson is a shipping clerk, his wife is in a millinery business, and they reside at 41 Kensington Gardens, Ilford. I stayed with them from June 18th 1921. The first week that I was there I was there as their guest and the remaining weeks I paid twenty five shillings a week. The cause of my leaving was that Mr Thompson quarrelled with Mrs Thompson and threw her across the room. I thought it was a very unmanly thing to do and I interfered. We had a quarrel and he asked me to leave and I left. I had always been exceedingly good friends with Mrs Thompson. I was also on visiting terms with the mother of Mrs Thompson, and family at 231 Shakespeare Crescent, Manor Park. After I left Mrs Thompson I went back to reside with my mother at present address. On the 7th September 1921 I got a position as a writer on board the S S Morea. I sailed on the 9th September and returned to England the end of the following month. Shortly after I came back from the voyage I called on Mr and Mrs Thompson at their address. Mrs Thompson received me quite friendly, Mr Thompson a little coldly, but we parted as friends. The same evening I called on Mrs Graydon and I there again saw Mr and Mrs Thompson who were visiting her. I have never called on Mr and Mrs Thompson since that time. I have met them once or twice at Mrs Graydon's since, the last time being in June last. Since that date I have never seen Mr Thompson. I have met Mrs Thompson on several occasions since and always by appointment. They were verbal appointments. On Monday last I met her by appointment at 12.30 at Aldersgate Street. We went to lunch at the Queen Anne's restaurant, Cheapside. After lunch she returned to business and I have not seen her since. Mr Thompson was not aware of our meeting, but some of them he was. I have known for a very long time past that she had led a very unhappy life with him. This is also known to members of Mrs Thompson's family. I have written to her on two separate occasions, I signed the letters Freddie and I addressed her as 'Dear Edie'. On the evening of Monday 2nd October I called on Mrs Graydon and stayed there till about 10 o'clock. I never mentioned the fact that I had lunch with Mrs Thompson that day, and as far as I know Mr Thompson was not aware of it. I left my house yesterday morning about a quarter to twelve. I was dressed in the same clothes that I am now wearing. I went up west and remained there until the evening. I was alone and never met anyone that I knew. I then went to Mrs Graydon's arriving there about 7. Left about 11 o'clock, my impression is that it had gone 11. Before leaving I remember Mrs Graydon's daughter Aviva saying that Percy (Mr Thompson) had phoned her up, I gathered from the observation she made that he was taking his wife to a theatre that night and that there was other members of the family going. When I left the house I went through Browning Road, into Sibley Grove to East Ham Railway Station. I booked to Victoria which is my usual custom.

I caught a train at 11.30 pm and I arrived at Victoria about 12.30 am. I then discovered that the last train to Gypsy Hill had gone, it leaves at 12.10 am. I had a few pounds in money with me but I decided to walk. I went by way of Vauxhall Road and Vauxhall Bridge, Brixton, turning to the left into Dulwich, and then onto the Crystal Palace and from there to my address at Upper Norwood arriving there about 3 am. I never noticed either bus or tram going in my direction. On arriving there I let myself in with a latch key and went straight to my bedroom. My mother called out to me. She said 'Is that you Mick?' I replied 'Yes' and then went to bed. I got up at about 9 am and about 12 I left home with my mother. I left my mother in Paternester Row about half-past two. I stayed in the city till about 5. I then went by train from Mark Lane to East Ham, and from there went to Mrs Graydon's arriving there about six. The first time that I learned Mr Thompson had been killed was when I bought a newspaper in Mark Lane before I got into the train to go to East Ham. I am never in the habit of carrying a knife, in fact I have never had one. I never met a single person that I knew from the time that I left Mrs Graydon's house until I arrived home. Mrs Thompson has written to me two or three times. I might have received one letter from her at home. The others I have received on board ship. I have destroyed these letters. She used to address me as 'Dear Freddie' and signed herself 'Peidi'. I occupy the backroom on the top floor at my address, and that is where I keep all my clothing. When I said I was dressed in precisely the same clothing yesterday as I am today, I meant it to include my undergarments with the exception of my collar and handkerchief which are at home."

Sellars continued with his evidence:

"Having made some further enquiries I again saw Bywaters on the evening of the 5th October, and said to him: I am going to charge you and Mrs Thompson with the wilful murder of Percy Thompson. He said 'Why her? Mrs Thompson was not aware of my movements.' I said 'If you wish to say anything I will take it down in writing.'"

After caution Bywaters made the following further statement:

"I wish to make a voluntary statement. Mrs Edith Thompson was not aware of my movements on Tuesday night, 3rd October. I left Manor Park at 11 pm and proceeded to Ilford. I waited for Mrs Thompson and her husband. When near Endsleigh Gardens I pushed her to one side, also pushing him further up the street. I said to him 'You have got to separate from your wife.' He said 'No' I said 'You will have to.' We struggled. I took my knife from my pocket and we fought and he got the worst of it. Mrs Thompson must have been spellbound for I saw nothing of her during the fight. I ran away through Endsleigh Gardens, through Wanstead, Leytonstone, Stratford, got a taxi at Stratford to Aldgate, walked from there to Fenchurch Street, got another taxi to Thornton Heath. Then walked to Upper Norwood arriving home about 3 am. The reason I fought with Thompson was because he never acted like a man to his wife. He always seemed several degrees lower than a snake. I loved her and I could not go on seeing her leading that life. I did not intend to kill him. I only meant to injure him. I gave him an opportunity of standing up to me as a man, but he wouldn't. I have had the knife some time; it was a sheath knife. I threw it down a drain when I was running through Endsleigh Gardens."

When charged Bywaters said. "It's wrong, it's wrong." Edith said nothing.

The only other evidence of significance was given by Dr Bernard Spilsbury. After describing the injuries caused to Percy Thompson by the knife, cross-examined by Sir Henry Curtis-Bennett he agreed that the *post mortem* revealed no trace of glass or poison having been administered.

CHAPTER 7

The Evidence of Frederick Bywaters and Edith Thompson

Cecil Whiteley, Bywaters counsel, was an able and experienced barrister. He had been a Treasury Counsel at the Old Bailey — that is to say one of the permanent advocates who present prosecution for the Crown at the Central Criminal Court. Yet on this occasion his task was impossible. He was defending a man whose only excuse for stabbing an unarmed man to death with a vicious weapon which he had been carrying was that he was acting in self-defence. No intelligent jury could accept such an absurdity.

But members of the English Bar are obliged in the course of their professional duty to put forward the defences which their clients instruct them to offer. It is closely allied to the 'cab rank' principle. A barrister is only entitled to refuse or return a brief in very exceptional circumstances — such as where the defendant virtually admits the offence, but nevertheless wishes to plead not guilty in the hope that the skill of counsel will enable him to escape justice.

Whiteley took Bywaters through the letters the best he could. Bywaters repetitiously claimed that references to poison and broken glass were regarded by himself as mere fantasising and that he never considered them as suggesting an attempt to kill or otherwise harm Percy Thompson. As to the passages in the letters which the Crown maintained were incitement to Bywaters to murder Thompson, Bywaters maintained that these referred to the possibilities for divorce or separation; a solution which would involve Edith obtaining employment abroad.

Three Cases that Shook the Law

The most crucial part of Bywaters evidence was when he was cross-examined by the Solicitor-General regarding the lead up to and the events during the assault on Percy Thompson.

> **Sir Thomas Inskip:** You met her at Fullers in the afternoon of the 3rd October?
> **Frederick Bywaters:** Yes.
> **Inskip:** Did you have any conversation about her husband?
> **Bywaters:** No.
> **Inskip:** Did you not refer to him?
> **Bywaters:** Only that she was going to the theatre.
> **Inskip:** Did she tell you that she was going to the theatre?
> **Bywaters:** Yes.
> **Inskip:** And she told you which theatre?
> **Bywaters:** Yes.
> **Inskip:** After you left her I understand you went straight to the Graydon's?
> **Bywaters:** Yes.
> **Inskip:** Were you carrying the knife when you went there?
> **Bywaters:** I was.
> **Inskip:** Did you carry the knife everywhere while in England?
> **Bywaters:** Yes.
> **Inskip:** Did you ever use it for anything?
> **Bywaters:** Cutting string or cutting things handy [the sheer absurdity of a man arming himself with sharp pointed stiletto type knife to cut string when a small pair of scissors will suffice to perform that function must have been apparent to the jury].
> **Inskip:** Is that the purpose for which you carried it?
> **Bywaters:** I thought that — it may be handy at any time.
> **Inskip:** A knife of that size and character?
> **Bywaters:** Yes, handy at sea.
> **Inskip:** Handy at sea. But was it handy at home?
> **Bywaters:** Yes.
> **Inskip:** As you told us, you knew before you went to the Graydon's that they were going to the theatre?
> **Bywaters:** Yes.

Inskip: When you made your statement of the 4th October did you say this?

"Before leaving I remember Mrs Graydon's daughter Avis saying that Percy [Thompson] had phoned her up, and I gathered from the observation he made that he was taking his wife to a theatre that night and that there were other members of the family going."

Inskip: You meant by that that you had heard it for the first time at the Graydon's?
Bywaters: I did not say.
Inskip: Did you mean that?
Bywaters: No, I meant what I say.
Inskip: Do you agree with me that the meaning of that paragraph is that you gathered it for the first time from conversation?
Bywaters: No.
Inskip: Just before that you say in your statement:

"I left my home yesterday morning about a quarter to twelve. I was dressed in the same clothes that I am now wearing. I was alone and never met anyone that I knew."

Inskip: That was untrue?
Bywaters: That was untrue. I objected to a lot of Superintendent Wensley's questions — I resented his questions.
Inskip: You mean by resented his questions that you told a falsehood?
Bywaters: Yes. I wanted to help Mrs Thompson.
Inskip: Did you tell falsehoods in order to shield yourself in that statement?
Bywaters: No.
Inskip: It was your one idea to shield Mrs Thompson?
Bywaters: That is so.
Inskip: Why did you not stick to your first statement? Why did you alter your statement?
Bywaters: I was told Mrs Thompson would be released if I made that statement.
Inskip: And you made the second statement?

Bywaters: I did.

Inskip: Was the second statement any more true than the first?

Bywaters: Yes.

Inskip: Did you say anything as to your meeting Mrs Thompson in your statement?

Bywaters: I don't know. What did I say?

Inskip: "Mrs Edith Thompson was not aware of my movements on Tuesday night 3rd October." At any rate whether you intended it or not, you did not correct your previous statement that you had not seen her on that day?

Bywaters: No.

Inskip: Why did you not put into your statement of the 5th October anything about the incident of the attack which you told us today? Had you forgotten that?

Bywaters: No. When I saw Mrs Thompson she was so ill I thought she was going to die, and I thought the sooner that I got it down the quicker she would be released and could go home with her mother.

Inskip: So you omitted that part of your story which was concerned with the threat to shoot and the struggle?

Bywaters: I did, that was my main object. I wanted to help her.

Inskip: Can you suggest how it helped her, to omit that important fact?

Bywaters: She would have been released. I did not trouble about details or anything like that. I had questions put to me and I said "yes". You say it?

Inskip: Was it true you said in your statement that you waited for Mrs Thompson and her husband?

Bywaters: No. That was untrue. I had that put to me.

Inskip: What you actually did was catch them up?

Bywaters: Yes. I overtook them.

Inskip: Are you a right handed or a left handed man?

Bywaters: Right.

Inskip: Did you strike the first blow from behind?

Bywaters: I struck the first blow in front, his right arm.

Inskip: Did the struggle take place at one spot, or was he moving forward?

Bywaters: I could not say whether we moved, I do not imagine we stood still.

Inskip: Did you say you remembered striking one blow at his throat?
Bywaters: I did not say that.
Inskip: Do you remember striking a blow at his throat?
Bywaters: I do not.
Inskip: And you do not remember anything, do you say, after you pushed Mrs Thompson away?
Bywaters: I remember pushing Thompson up the street, and the conversation between us, and the subsequent events.
Inskip: Did you not discuss in the Tea Room that afternoon the possibility of meeting them that night?
Bywaters: We did not stay in the Tea Room. She did not come into the Tea Room; I left it to join her.
Inskip: Did you not discuss with her something desperate?
Bywaters: I did not.
Inskip: Did you not refer to her husband except in connection with the theatre party?
Bywaters: That is the only way we referred to him.
Inskip: Did she tell you she had abandoned all ideas of suicide?
Bywaters: No.
Inskip: Did she make any reference to poison, or force or violence?
Bywaters: She did not.
Inskip: And your story is that you went out from the Graydon's never intending to use violence on Mr Thompson?
Bywaters: I never intended to see them when I first went out.
Inskip: You formed your idea on your way home from the station at West Ham?
Bywaters: East Ham.
Inskip: Is this true in your second statement "I only meant to injure him"?
Bywaters: It is hardly true. I meant to stop him from killing me.
Inskip: "I did not intend to kill him. I only meant to injure him." Is that true. That you went there to injure him?
Bywaters: No sir it is not.
Inskip: "I gave him the opportunity of standing up to me as a man, but he would not." Was that true?

Bywaters: When I said that I referred to a back occasion, not to this occasion.

Inskip: Did you on this occasion give him the opportunity of standing up to you as a man?

Bywaters: No. I did not suggest any violence or fisticuffs at all.

Inskip: Do you mean you suggest that he made the first assault upon you.

Bywaters: Yes. He did.

Inskip: And that you drew your knife?

Bywaters: I did.

Inskip: Is it the fact that you never saw any revolver or any gun at that moment?

Bywaters: I never saw it, no.

Inskip: Did you continue to stab him in the expectation of seeing one at any moment?

Bywaters: I did not know I was stabbing him. I tried to stop him from shooting me; that is all.

In re-examination Cecil Whitely did his best to repair the damage, but the absurdity of Bywaters account of how Thompson received his injuries which resulted in his death had rendered Whiteley's task impossible.

The point in the trial was now reached where Sir Henry Curtis-Bennett had to decide whether or not to call his client to give evidence on her own behalf. This is a grave decision for counsel for the defence, especially in a case where the life of the defendant hangs on the result of the trial. There are two courses of action available. One is not to call the defendant into the witness box and to effectively say to the prosecution—you have brought this case, now you have to prove it. The other is to call the defendant and let him or her tell their own story to the court. Both have their dangers.

If the accused person fails to testify the jury may take the view that his or her failure to do so is an indication of guilt—otherwise why are they hesitant about telling their side of the story.

On the other hand if the person on trial does give evidence they may perform disastrously under cross-examination and hence give the impression of dishonesty and duplicity. A further consideration is that if evidence is called for the defence the right of having the last word with the jury is lost.

Curtis-Bennett must have endured much heart-searching over this issue, but in fact the decision was made for him by Edith herself. She was determined that the court should hear her side of the matter. Sir Henry tried desperately to dissuade her from doing so. He was certain, correctly as it turned out, that she would make a bad impression on the jury. He had endeavoured to create a picture of a woman who was a fantasist, remarkable in many ways and unbalanced in her affections but no murderer. His whole strategy was to show that the charge she faced was the wrong one for which there was no evidence. But he was alive to the faults of his client. In the event she proved to be a conceited and self-centred woman whose word was not to be trusted. The impression she made on the court was well-nigh disastrous.

In her evidence in chief she said that her marriage was not a happy one and that although she had begged her husband to agree to a separation he would not do so. She insisted that she had never administered poison or broken glass to Percy. Mr Frampton, Sir Henry's junior, then turned to the letters.

Questioned about the passage in the letter of 20th August 1921 — "Come and see me Monday lunchtime, please darlint. He suspects." Edith replied:

"I mean that my husband suspected I had seen Bywaters; I think it was on the Friday previous to that date. I usually saw him on Fridays and I continued to see him until he sailed on the 9th September. He came back in the end of October, and remained in this country until the 11th November. After he sailed I corresponded with him and among other letters I wrote Exhibit 62 which is undated.

All I could think of last night was that compact we made. Shall we have to carry it through. Don't let us darlint. I'd like to live and be happy — not for a little while, but for the while you still love me. Death seemed horrible last night — when you think about it darlint, it does seem a horrible thing to die. When you have never been happy really happy for one little minute."

Frampton: What compact were you referring to in that letter to Bywaters?

Edith Thompson: The compact of suicide. We had discussed the question of suicide sometime previous to the writing of this letter; I cannot state when.

Frampton: What was said about it?

Thompson: That nothing was worth living for, and that it would be far easier to be dead.

Frampton: Had you discussed any particular means of committing suicide?

Thompson: I believe we had.

Frampton: After Bywaters had sailed on that voyage did you send him from time to time cuttings out of the papers?

Thompson: I did — they were generally cuttings that I sent. There was an account of an inquest on a girl Freda Kempton, who had died through taking an overdose of cocaine.

Frampton: In your letter of the 14th March 1922 (Exhibit 20) you say: "Enclosed are some cuttings that may be interesting. I think the red hair one is true in parts — you tell me which parts darlint. The Kempton cutting may be interesting if it's to be the same method". What were you referring to there?

Thompson: Our compact of suicide.

Edith admitted that she and Bywaters had talked about giving Thompson something to make him ill. In answer to the judge's question — "Do you mean you had talked about poison?" she replied "I do not mean anything in particular." She insisted that she had never given him anything. She was taken to the letter (Exhibit 27):

"[Y]ou know darlint I am beginning to think I have gone wrong in the way I manage this affair. I think perhaps it would have been better had I acquiesced in everything he said and did or wanted to do. At least it would have disarmed any suspicion he might have had and that would have been better if we have to use drastic measures."

Mr Frampton: What were you meaning by the "drastic measure" you might have to use?

> **Thompson:** Leaving England with Bywaters.
>
> **Frampton:** Turn now to your letter of 10th February (Exhibit 15). "Darlint—you must do something this time—I am not really impatient—but opportunities come and go by—they have to—because I'm helpless and I think and think and think—perhaps it will never come again". What did you mean by "you must do something this time"?
>
> **Thompson:** I meant he must find me some sort of situation or take me away altogether without one. I had discussed the question of Bywaters finding me a situation and also the place where he was to look for one for me—in Bombay, Marseilles, Australia—in fact really anywhere where he heard of anything.

Time and again Edith explained that compromising passages in her letters were only intended to retain Bywaters' affections. She was referring only, she said, to the possibility of their eloping or at least of Frederick finding her employment in another country. But her answers were becoming less and less plausible.

> **Frampton:** I am going to try the glass again occasionally—when it is safe—I've put in an electric light bulb this time." What did you mean Bywaters to understand by that?
>
> **Thompson:** That I was willing to help him in whatever he wanted me to do or suggested I should do or we should do. There were electric light bulbs in the house.
>
> **Frampton:** Had you an electric light bulb for any purpose of this description?
>
> **Thompson:** I had not.
>
> **Frampton:** Did you ever intend to use one?
>
> **Thompson:** I did not.
>
> **Frampton:** Did you ever or at any time use one?
>
> **Thompson:** Never.

Could Edith expect the jury to take replies like these seriously?

Then, in total contradiction to the foregoing came the following: "I used the light bulb three times, but the third time he found a piece—so I have given it up until you come home."

Edith was then questioned regarding passages in the letter written after 19th September 1922 (Exhibit 28):

> "Yes darlint you are jealous of him—but I want you to be—he has the right by law to all that you have the right to by nature and love—yes darlint be jealous, so much that you will do something desperate."

Frampton: What do you mean by doing something desperate?
Thompson: To take me away at any cost, to do anything to take me away from England.

Then came the letter (Exhibit 60) written shortly before the murder took place. It contained this passage:

> "Darlint, do something tomorrow night will you? Something to make you forget. I'll be hurt I know, but I want you to hurt me—I do really—the bargain now seems so one sided—so unfair but how can I alter it?"

Frampton: Tomorrow night, was the night you were going to the theatre, what had Bywaters to forget?
Thompson: That I was going somewhere with my husband.

Questioned about the discussion in the Tea Room Edith simply said that it had concerned freedom.

In her testimony regarding the murder Edith failed to disclose that the assailant was Bywaters.

When Sir Thomas Inskip rose to cross-examine it was already clear that Edith in the witness box had been a complete disaster. Her blithe dismissals of those passages most undermining of her defence, on the grounds that she was merely trying to keep the affections of her lover, made a bad impression on the jury. So bad in fact that the Solicitor-General's task had virtually been done for him.

Inskip's very first question related to the moment of Percy's murder.

Sir Thomas Inskip: Have you any recollection now of what happened when your husband was killed?

Edith Thompson: Except what I have said, I was dazed.

Inskip: Is exhibit four, the short statement, everything you remembered and is it true? Was the statement you made to the police, which I will read to you, your recollection at the time, or was it deliberately untrue?

[The statement was read out]

Inskip: Now did you intend to tell an untruth then about the incident?

Thompson: Yes.

Inskip: Was that to shield Bywaters?

Thompson: It was.

Inskip: In your statement you say: We were coming along Belgrave Road and just past the corner of Endsleigh Gardens when I heard him call out "ooer" and he fell up against me. Does that not suggest that he was taken ill, and that nobody was present?

Thompson: Yes.

Inskip: Did you intend, when you said that, to tell an untruth?

Thompson: It was an untruth.

Inskip: And you intended it to be an untruth?

Thompson: I did, but I did not mean it was an untruth that he said "ooer" and fell up against me.

Inskip: It is an untruth in so far as it suggests that that was the first thing that happened?

Thompson: That is so.

Inskip: Was that again to shield Bywaters?

Thompson: It was.

Inskip: At the time you made this statement to the police you knew it was Bywaters who had done it?

Thompson: I did. I do not know what you mean by "done it". I did not know then that anything was actually done. When I say I knew it was Bywaters, I mean that I recognised his coat and his hat going away.

Further pressed in cross-examination Edith admitted she saw her husband and the other man scuffling. This was inconsistent with an earlier statement she made that someone flew past. She knew it was Bywaters when he started to move away.

Regarding her marriage Edith said she was never happy with her husband and wanted to divorce him. She said she had told her husband that she had been unfaithful to him with Bywaters.

Her admissions, although reluctant, were damaging when they came. She had urged Bywaters to send her something to make her husband ill. She did not discourage him from sending it. She agreed that she was acting towards Bywaters in a way that showed that she wished to destroy her husband's life.

She parried most of the questions regarding the letters with the oft repeated reply that these were an invention to impress Bywaters.

In re-examination Curtis-Bennett was very brief. His client had stood her ground, but the impression of a less than credit worthy unrepentant adulteress weighed heavily with the judge and jury.

CHAPTER 8

The Closing Speeches of Counsel

Cecil Whiteley did his best for Bywaters, but it was a lost cause—and he knew it. The savagery of the knife attack on Percy Thompson ruled out any question of self-defence. Even had there been an element of provocation, which is doubtful, Bywaters admitted drawing the knife without having seen any weapon in the hands of Percy.

The final projection in Whiteley's speech to the jury is, however, worthy of repetition:

> "Judge this young man as you yourself would be judged. One life has been sacrificed already in this sordid and horrible drama. Is there to be yet another? Frederick Bywaters makes his last appeal to you through me and he says to you 'it is true, only too true that I have been weak, extremely weak. It is true, only too true, that I allowed myself to drift into this dishonourable entanglement and intrigue with a married woman living with her husband. It is true that I had not the moral courage to cut myself adrift from it and end it all. It is true, only too true, that she confided in me, that I was flattered that she should come to me a young man of nineteen and confide in me. It is true that I pitied her and my pity turned to love. I did not realise, I did not know, I had not enough experience in this life to know that true love must mean self-sacrifice.' All this is true, he says, but I ask you to believe and by your verdict to proclaim to the whole world that in all this history I am not an assassin, I am not a murderer."

The jury did not comply with counsel's request.

Sir Henry Curtis-Bennett rose to address the jury, looking as usual his impressive and confident self. That confidence may have been diminished by the performance of his client in the witness box. He began by emphasising the essence of the charge in the indictment which Edith Thompson faced. Namely, that she was not merely present at the murder of Thompson but aiding and abetting it. He pointed out that other charges in the second indictment were not proceeded with. The jury, he stressed were not concerned with those other offences of conspiracy to murder; soliciting to murder, inciting to commit a misdemeanour; administering poison with intent to murder and administering a destructive thing with intent to murder. The prosecution had chosen to put before the court the case that she assisted Bywaters in the murder and it was their duty to prove it if they could. This was the crux of the case against Edith, and Curtis-Bennett was right to emphasise it at the start of his address: By the prosecution it is stated that Mrs Thompson was what is known in the law as a principal in the second degree, namely a person who "aids, abets or assists a murderer when he is committing a murder."

At this point Mr Justice Shearman intervened. This was only one of the judge's interjections which indicates his hostility towards the defendant.

> **Mr Justice Shearman:** That is not exclusive. If two people contrive a murder they are guilty of murder, even though one was not there.
>
> **Sir Henry Curtis-Bennett:** Yes, he is an accessory.
>
> **Shearman:** You say he is not guilty of murder if he did not actually take part in it.
>
> **Curtis-Bennett:** I am not going to shirk any issue. It is no good when representing somebody to try and put before the jury some story which does not meet the case at all. It cannot be alleged that anything further might be charged against her.
>
> **Shearman:** Of course a person might be regarded as an accessory before the fact.
>
> **Curtis-Bennett:** If the case as suggested by the prosecution were that Mrs Thompson knew what was going to happen that night, and that she took the person who was going to be murdered to the spot where he was murdered, then I would welcome that case. The jury would see that the

whole of the evidence was to the contrary in such a case. If you come to the conclusion that she conspired with Bywaters to murder her husband on that night, then you will convict from that indictment if you are satisfied that she was urging on Bywaters at this moment. However, she sits in the dock charged with being a murderess on the night of the 3rd October and it is for the prosecution to satisfy you that she is guilty. I suppose that the case for the prosecution is founded upon nothing but these letters written over a period of time, and founded outside that on nothing but guesswork, contradicted when you come to test it. I suppose the case is that there was an arrangement upon that night that Mr Thompson should be murdered, that Mrs Thompson was a party to it, and that Mrs Thompson knew quite well as she was walking down the road near her home that at any moment her husband was going to be taken from her side and murdered in cold blood. I contend that every single action of Mrs Thompson on the night when the killing took place shows that she knew nothing of what was going to happen.

Sir Henry has taken a strong stand on the law relating to his client. But from that point onwards his tactics were totally flawed. His appeal to the jury was far too theatrical, almost sentimental. He painted a picture of a love affair with overtones of Heloise and Abelard; Romeo and Juliet:

"You have got to get into the atmosphere of this case, this is no ordinary case you are trying. These are not ordinary people that you are trying. This is not an ordinary charge against ordinary people. It is very difficult to get into the atmosphere of a play or opera, but you have to do it in this case. Am I right or wrong in saying that this woman is one of the most extraordinary personalities that you or I have ever met?"

Counsel dealt with Edith's absorption with novels. Then he continued:

"You have read her letters. Have you ever read mixed up with criticism of books, mixed up with all sorts of references with which I shall have to deal, more beautiful language of love? Such things have very seldom been put by pen upon paper. This is the woman you have to deal with, not some ordinary woman. She is one of those striking personalities met with from time to time who stand out for some reason or another."

How could such a distinguished and experienced advocate as Curtis-Bennett have so badly misjudged the atmosphere of the court and the practical, down to earth common sense of a London jury. Surely he might have guessed that they would find the "beautiful language of love" nauseating. The judge himself referred to it as gush. Mistake was compounded by further error when he spoke of the great love between the defendants. To describe an underhanded intrigue which led to murder in such terms was bound to weaken the whole of Sir Henry's address. How could the court trust her plea that she was only trying to avoid losing her lover and not inciting him to kill her husband. To compare the incriminating passages in the letters with mere loose exaggerated talk sometimes engaged in by people was frankly absurd.

If, as Sir Henry admitted, Edith was prepared to tell any lie to keep her lover where does that leave her credibility?

Even counsel's warning to the jury not to convict his client for her lack of morals went down badly:

> "I ask you again to get into the atmosphere of the life of Mrs Thompson. I do not care whether it is described as an amazing passion, to use the expression of the Solicitor-General, or as an adulterous intercourse. Thank God, this is not a court of morals, because if everybody immoral was brought here I would never be out of it, nor would you. Whatever name is given to it, it was certainly a great love that existed between these two people."

Curtis-Bennett rightly placed emphasis on the evidence of Dr Spilsbury and Mr Webster to the effect that, resulting from the *post-mortem* there was no trace of glass or poison having been given to Percy Thompson. But if Edith in her letters had told Bywaters that she had administered these things that could act as an enticement, even if it was a lie.

When the time came for the adjournment Curtis Bennet was still part way through his speech. The judge then made a very unusual intervention which might more properly have been reserved for his summing-up:

"Before the court rises I wish to offer you, members of the jury, this advice. Of course you will not make up your minds until you have heard the whole case. The only other thing is, having regard to the surroundings for so many days, by all means look at the atmosphere and try to understand what the letters mean. But you should not forget that you are in a court of justice trying a vulgar and common crime. You are not listening to a play from the stalls of the theatre. When you are thinking it over you should think it over in that way."

That intrusion by the judge was devastating to the tenor of Sir Henry's plea. He realised this, and at the following session of the court concentrated on the points which were more strongly favourable to the defence.

Dealing with the letters he emphasised the words regarding the time limits agreed. "We have only three and a half years left darlint, try and help, Peidi?" "It is almost inconceivable," said Sir Henry, "that it can be suggested on that letter, or to think seriously that the prosecution can say it shows that those two persons were plotting murder. The words show quite the contrary. Do you imagine that a woman who at that time, according to the prosecution, had got to the degree of having incited this man to the extent that murder is imminent would be writing 'we have only three and a half years left?' Do you think you would find in these letters some references egging on, inciting, soliciting, Bywaters to commit this murder? Yet you find in my submission exactly the opposite. There is not one reference in these letters which any one in this court dare say shows that the suggestion made by the prosecution is true."

Curtis-Bennett then turned to the passage regarding funds. "I tried to find a way out of tonight darlingest. We must make a study of this deceit for some time longer … Until we have funds we can do nothing."

"Do the prosecution," Curtis-Bennett, asked, "say that this letter on October the second is evidence that these two people are intending murder next day, or the day after, or the week after? She is saying till we have funds we can do nothing. They did not want funds for murder. But it was essential they should have funds for living together. Mrs Thompson said that if she were to run away with Bywaters as she wanted to she would have to leave her business. 'Darlingest, find me a job abroad'. Murderess, say the prosecution."

Counsel for the defence then spoke of the conversation in the Tea Room in which the prosecution claimed murder was planned. That claim was totally unjustified. There was no evidence to support it.

With regard to the attack on Thompson by Bywaters, Curtis-Bennett emphasised what should have already been clear to the court—all the signs were that it came as a complete surprise to her and that she showed genuine shock and dismay.

The Solicitor-General was brief in his final address. Under prompting from the Judge, Inskip defined the prosecution argument in a manner which came close to stating the case for the defence:

> "I am not going to suggest that merely because some foolish or wild expressions were used in the letters it is sufficient for you to say that in consequence of the fact the murder was committed Mrs Thompson is guilty. I agree with my learned friend for the defence that in order for you to arrive at a verdict of murder against Mrs Thompson you must be satisfied that the persuasion lasted right up to the murder and was the continuing cause in consequence of which the murder was committed. If you think that the persuasion had no real connection with the murder and that the expressions, however criminal and foolish, were not really the cause of the murder, then of course it was not a case of murder against Mrs Thompson. What I ask you to consider is the progress of the idea found in the letters and to see how it was pressed by Mrs Thompson on Bywaters and how the idea continued right up to the last moment."

Inskip pressed the case for the Crown no further. He had no need to, the judge did it for him.

CHAPTER 9

The Summing-up

One thing is certain regarding the summing-up of Mr Justice Shearman. As previously indicated this judge was a clever and gifted member of the judiciary. He was no novice at bringing his influence to bear upon a jury.

The law for judges in England in a criminal trial is different from that in the United States of America. In both countries the law is the province of the judge and the facts are solely the concern of the jury.

However this rule is interpreted more strictly in America. Unlike his American counterpart an English judge is entitled to comment on the facts and, depending on the individual judge concerned, this may amount to a clear direction in favour of a conviction or an acquittal or perhaps just a gentle nudge in the direction which the judge would like the jury to go. Yet although the judge, within the limits of judicial impartiality, is entitled to bring to bear a degree of influence upon the jury he will wisely avoid exercising this prerogative too freely. If he or she is not careful he or she may provoke the members of the jury into returning a very different verdict from the one intended. Juries do not take kindly to a blatantly biased figure on the bench.

Mr Justice Shearman undoubtedly harboured a bias against Edith Thompson. But it was a bias which found expression by laying emphasis on those points which were favourable to the prosecution case while disposing lightly with the material upon which the arguments for the defence rested.

The judge commenced his address by stating a principle of law with which no lawyer on either side could quarrel:

"Now I am going to ask you to consider only one question in your deliberations and that is; was it an arranged thing between the woman and the man?" If he had adhered to this statement of the meaning of aiding and abetting the judge might well have directed the jury for an acquittal, since all the evidence—apart from mere conjecture—pointed to the conclusion that there was no prior arrangement between Edith and Bywaters that Thompson was to be murdered—that, or any other night. Having given some obvious examples of what constitutes aiding and abetting Shearman continued: "But I do not think it is quite the case you have to consider here. At half past five she leaves him (Bywaters) telling him where she is going and that she is coming back with her husband in the evening. If you think it was no surprise to her when she saw him there that evening, and if you think that when she saw him that evening he came there under her direction, with the hand that she was guiding. If you think he had that knife in his pocket intending to murder—of course this only arises if you think he had that knife in his pocket intending to murder that man that evening—and if you think she knew that he had it I think it necessarily follows that she would know that he was going to do it that evening. This is what I submit to you. Therefore I think the only case I am going to ask you to consider is this, was she already party to the murder in that sense. That she was aiding and abetting it? The words are pretty plain 'aiding and abetting' means giving a help to the murderer, if it actually took place."

No criticism can be made regarding the judge's direction on aiding and abetting. What appears unjust and unmerited is the way in which he appears to make assumptions, and plants these in the minds of the jury, which are wholly unsupported by the evidence. The fact that Bywaters knew Edith was going to the theatre that evening is no necessary indication that the spot where the murder took place and the time had been agreed between himself and Edith. The dogmatic manner in which Mr Justice Shearman put the prosecution case to the jury may well have created the impression in their minds that this was the only reasonable solution.

It must be remembered that the authority of the judge, particularly a judge of the High Court, carried a great weight of authority at this period. Nowhere in his summing-up did the judge pay anything like the attention to the defence as he bestowed on the Crown case. Indeed there are passages in which the judge puts the prosecution case more effectively than Sir Thomas Inskip. Having done so Mr Justice Shearman is careful to cover his tracks with phrases such as "of course gentlemen, the conclusion which you reach is entirely for you." He even warns them against thinking he is taking sides.

Dealing with the correspondence Shearman places great emphasis upon those letters in which there is reference to broken glass and poison. The later correspondence in which Edith asks Bywaters to find her a job abroad and speaks of them only having three and a quarter years left receive not a mention. Perhaps however, more remarkable, is the manner in which the judge almost brushed aside a piece of evidence which rang true and if correct threw a spanner into the prosecution case regarding the alleged co-operation between Edith and Frederick in the murder of Percy Thompson. The passage in the summing-up reads as follows with the present author's comments inserted in square brackets:

> "There is one other very curious piece of evidence to which I want to call your attention, and that is the evidence of Mr Webber. He says he heard a noise, and these are his words, he heard these words—'Oh don't, oh don't' in piteous tones. You know he is some way off. I am not saying it is true [Why should Webber lie?], it is for you to say whether it is accurate, or whether it is imaginary or whether he has made a mistake [Why?] but there is the evidence. The voice was Mrs Thompson's [This concession destroys the judge's caveats]. 'It was three or four minutes before I came out, and then I heard the doctor ask had he been ill. Now of course it is for you to say if you believe that [Why not believe it?] what the words mean 'oh don't, oh don't' in piteous tones, and it is made use of by counsel as showing that she objected to the murder and was saying 'don't.' Well a remark of force, but it is a double edged weapon, this evidence, if you think it is accurate, because if you think it means that when she saw him being stabbed or saw one of the stabs she said don't don't it means that she was looking on and saw it all.

The evidence is incompatible with the story that she was senseless and only recovered — you know her story, I need not go into that matter again — if she was pushed aside and damaged by a fall, and there is independent evidence that she had a bruise. That does not prove how the bruise was given but her story is that she knew nothing of it. She saw some scuffling a little way down, and she saw the back of a man running away, knowing who he was. Of course if that is so, it is impossible that she could be saying 'don't don't' [Why?] and she saw the blows struck. I think it is entirely for you — I will not argue that."

There are two defects in this passage in the judge's direction to the jury. Firstly, it is not consistent with the evidence and secondly it constitutes a non sequitur in her further statement to Richard Sellars. Edith did not say she was knocked senseless and therefore knew nothing of how she received the bruise. Hence the conclusion of the judge that she could not have called out 'oh don't' because she would not have seen the attack is a false assumption. Her statement reads as follows:

"When we got near Endsleigh Gardens a man rushed out from the gardens and knocked me away from my husband. I was dazed for a moment. When I recovered I saw my husband scuffling with a man. The man who I knew as Freddie Bywaters was running away. He was wearing a blue overcoat and a grey hat. I knew it was him although I did not see his face."

This makes it plain that Edith had ample time to cry out 'oh don't, oh don't'. The fact that she failed at first to name Bywaters as the assailant is perfectly explicable on the basis of a love-struck woman attempting to protect her paramour. When wiser counsels prevailed she named him. This alternative scenario was never properly put to the jury — or for that matter put at all.

Mr Justice Shearman concluded with these words:

"Gentlemen, that is really the whole of the case. I ask your earnest consideration of it. I am not going to say another word to you about the case of the man, only to repeat that if you find the man guilty of murder, then you have to consider, was this woman an active party to it, did she direct him to go; did she know he was coming; are you satisfied that she was implicated directly in it? Her story is that she knew nothing about it, it was a surprise, in fact she was pushed aside and she immediately fainted. She did not know what was going on, when a man pushed her against the wall she did not look up to see what happened, she swooned away, and then at the end she sees Bywaters going away. You know exactly what was done before the act; you know the facts of all the letters; and you know what she did after, and you know that her evidence is now that she knew nothing about it. In the letters she was merely saying that she was poisoning her husband in order to make an appearance before Bywaters. Her whole case is, she says, she was quite innocent of this matter, and that she is shocked at everything that happened and had nothing to do with it. You will not convict her unless you are satisfied that she and he agreed that this man should be murdered when he could be, and she knew he was going to do it, and directed him to do it and by arrangement between them he was doing it. If you are satisfied of that it will be your duty to convict her. Will you please retire and consider your verdict."

Both defendants were found guilty of murder.

The case went on appeal to the Court of Criminal Appeal. The Lord Chief Justice, Lord Hewart, delivered the judgement of the court.

He outlined the circumstances in which the murder took place. Then he turned to the letters.

"With regard to the letters in the opinion of this court there was more than one ground upon which the use of these letters could be justified. It is enough for the present purpose to say that they could be justified upon this ground—that by means of them the prosecutors were seeking to show that continuously over a long period beginning before and culminating in the time antecedent to the commission of the crime, Mrs Thompson was, with every sort of ingenuity, by precept and by example, actual or simulated endeavouring to incite Bywaters, to the commission of this crime. I am not going to read those letters. There is a great mass of them.

M for murder by poisoning any of them were unread at the trial. They begin in the summer of 1921 and they continue until the 2nd October 1922, that is to say, they continue until the day before the day upon which this crime was committed. Now what is it that those letters may reasonably be regarded as showing?

First of all they show a passionate, and in the circumstances a wicked affection between Mrs Thompson and Bywaters. Secondly, they contain what purports to be accounts of efforts which had been made, sometimes without the assistance of Bywaters, sometimes with the assistance of Bywaters, to get Mr Thompson out of the way. Thirdly, and this is the thread which runs through the whole skin of those letters, there is the continued entreaty and hope that that which they both desire will somehow be accomplished. Now, in the opinion of the court, the theory that these letters so far as they purport to describe attempts made upon the life of Mr Thompson are mere nonsense—'vapour' as Bywater calls them, melodramatic nonsense as counsel has thought fit to call them, is a theory which cannot be accepted.

But however that may be, if the question is, as I think it was, whether these letters were evidence of a protracted continuous incitement to Bywaters to commit the crime which he did in the end commit it really is of comparatively little importance. There the appellant was truly reporting something which she had done, or falsely reporting something which she merely pretended to do. I am not going to read them, it is not necessary, but reference may perhaps be made to one of them, which is the last. By this time Bywaters was back in the country, the appellant and Bywaters were meeting. They had ample opportunity of conversation and arrangement of any plan in which they might be interested, and upon the 2nd October the appellant wrote to him—'I tried so hard to find a way out of tonight darlingst, but he was suspicious and still is…We ought to be able to use great big things for great big love like ours.' And again 'Darlingst it is fundings that are our stumbling block—until we have those, we can do nothing'.

That is not the only passage in the later correspondence in which the appellant refers to the importance of money. Then she goes on 'Darlingst, do

The Summing-up

something tomorrow night will you? Something to make you forget. I'll be hurt I know, but I want you to hurt me—I do really—the bargain now seems so one sided—so unfair—but how can I alter it.' And finally the last passage 'Don't forget when we talked in the Tea Room. I'll still risk and try if you will—we only have 3 ¾ years left darlingst.'

Now it cannot be said that those letters were not evidence against the appellant in support of the charge which the prosecution were making up against her."

The prevailing view of an appeal against conviction during that era was that the jury had heard the case, had seen the defendant giving evidence and being cross-examined and were the best judges of the truthfulness of him or her. Indeed it was not until the Wallace case at Liverpool in 1931 that for the first time the Court of Criminal Appeal reversed the verdict of a jury.

This appears plainly from the concluding words of the Lord Chief Justice, Lord Hewart:

"Taking that summing-up as a whole, and reading one part with the rest of what the learned judge says in the opinion of this court it is not possible to found upon it any unfavourable criticism. The case was clearly put before the jury. There was simple evidence, partly direct evidence, partly evidence from which inference might properly be drawn; and upon that evidence is a case which exhibits from beginning to end no redeeming feature, the members of the jury have convicted the appellant; in the opinion of this court there is no reason to interfere with that conviction, and this appeal must be dismissed."

Perhaps the final word rests with Filson Young in his introduction to the trial of Bywaters and Thompson in the *Notable British Trials* series.

"Age is eternally jealous of youth, impotence is jealous of passion; love is jealous of liberty; those who have found happiness within the pale are apt to look with suspicion and misgivings on those who dare to seek and find happiness without the pale. Intellect affects to despise emotion; yet a real and deep emotion, however wayward, is a more vital thing than are the sterile and negative barriers within which, necessarily but in vain, the social state tries to confine it. That is why we have courts of law for a world ruled only by emotion would be a dreadful place. The lesson of it all is surely never to let emotion escape from its own sphere, to wander into the dreadful wilderness that ends in the court and the prison house. Mr Justice Shearman frequently referred to Bywaters as 'the adulterer' apparently quite unconscious of the fact that to people of Bywaters generation educated in the ethics of dear labour and cheap pleasure, of the commercial sport and the dancing hall adultery is merely a quaint ecclesiastical term for what seems to them the great adventure of their lives. Adultery to such people may or may not be 'sporting' but its wrongness is not a matter that would trouble them for a moment. Sinai for them is wrapped in impenetrable cloud. And if we are not prepared to adapt the laws of Sinai to the principles of the night club and the dansant I see no other alternative, but to educate our young in the eternal verities on which the law is based."

CHAPTER 10

The Final Tragedy

In his summing-up to the jury the trial judge put the case against Edith fairly and squarely:

> "If you think it was no surprise to her when she saw him that evening, and if you think that when she saw him there that evening he came there under her direction under her information that she would be there about that time, and that he was waiting there for their arrival under her direction and information that she had given him as to where she would be about that time — if you think she knew perfectly well as soon as she set eyes on him that he was there to murder, she is guilty of the murder too, because he was doing it under her direction with the hand that she was guiding."

This direction by Mr Justice Shearman cannot be faulted. It encapsulated the issue which came before the Court of Criminal Appeal on the 21st December 1922, namely was the murder of Percy Thompson on the 3rd October 1922 planned between Edith Thompson and Frederick Bywaters.

The prosecution had, at the start of the case, clearly accepted the dearth of evidence, both before and after the murder, of any such plan. They sought to make good this weakness by introducing the element of incitement, notwithstanding the fact that no charge of incitement had been proceeded with. The letters alleged to amount to this offence dated from months before the event. Two dubious propositions were advanced to support each other.

The Lord Chief Justice, giving reason for the court's decision said:

"There was no direct evidence that he was there at her initiation, or upon information given by her. That is quite true. But in view of all the rest of the evidence, both as to what happened before the commission of those acts, and as to what happened immediately after the commission of those acts, it was obviously open to the jury to infer that that which was done was done as the result of a preconcerted arrangement, and that is what the learned judge is putting her, making it plain again and again that they must be satisfied before they draw that inference."

Only twice before in 1931 had appeals against the death sentence been upheld in the Court of Criminal Appeal since it had had been set up in 1907. The first of these was on the grounds that the judge had misdirected the jury. The second because the defence had not been properly presented at the trial. Only in the *Wallace* case in which the appellant William Herbert Wallace was appealing against a conviction for the murder of his wife Julia, did the appeal judges declare that the jury had made a mistake.

The appeal for clemency to Home Secretary William Bridgeman failed and Edith was executed. Her hanging and, over 30 years later in 1955, that of Ruth Ellis, were instrumental in bringing about the abolition of capital punishment in the United Kingdom. Not least in this were stories of disturbing scenes surrounding the death of Thompson as to which the official documents and papers remain closed. But it is on record that executioner John Ellis eventually committed suicide after stating that the events haunted him.

PART 2
WILLIAM JOYCE

Three Cases that Shook the Law

CHAPTER 11

The Trial of William Joyce: Introduction

The trial of William Joyce contrasts sharply with that of Edith Thompson. She was wrongly executed because the jury, under the influence of Mr Justice Shearman, decided upon wholly insufficient evidence, that she was present aiding and abetting the murder of her husband Percy. William Joyce met a similar fate because the law of treason in England was artificially extended to a point far beyond what had been intended by its original framers.

It had long been the law that actions injurious to the British Crown committed abroad in time of war were only justiciable in the courts of this country if perpetrated by a British citizen. An exemption to this rule had to be found if William Joyce, otherwise known as Lord Haw-Haw, could be brought to justice to answer for his many broadcasts to England made during the hostilities from 1940 to 1945.

In fairness to the authorities there is little doubt that the release of Joyce would have provoked an outcry. The fact that he soon became a figure of fun with his strange pseudo-educated English accent and his not infrequent prophecies of doom for an England which had dared to stand up to the Third Reich, which failed to materialise, did not alter the position. Treason, if such it was, so persistent and prolonged called out for retribution. That was certainly the view of the average English citizen at that time.

Let us, first of all, take a look at this rather strange figure, now a forgotten remnant of the Second World War, but whose trial will long be remembered in the annals of the law of high treason in this country.

William Joyce was born in Heikemer Street in Brooklyn, New York to an English mother and an Irish Roman Catholic father who had taken United States citizenship. These facts far from being of ancillary interest, pervade the whole of the subsequent story, for it was certain evidence that Joyce was an American and not a British citizen. This fact was not known to the authorities until the charge of treason was brought against him. Then it was of the greatest embarrassment to the prosecuting authorities who had assumed he was a British citizen. A few years after he was born, the Joyce family returned to Galway, Ireland, where Joyce attended the Jesuit College of St Ingnatious. Joyce, like his father, was a strong Unionist, and as such claimed that he was a target for the IRA. He came to England and attended an English school. His family followed two years later. He applied to Birkbeck College at the University of London where he obtained a first class degree. He developed an interest in Fascism and gave assistance to a Fascist group.

In 1924 he received a scar on his right cheek due to a battle, he alleged, with some Jewish Communists.

In 1932 he joined the British Union of Fascists. He acquired a reputation as a brawler and having joined the BUF under Sir Oswald Mosley, he made a name for himself as a speaker. However, the violence of his attacks, verbal and physical, upon opponents began to marginalise the BUF and in 1937 he was sacked by Mosley.

After he had been expelled Joyce formed his own group the National Socialist League and concentrated on anti-Semitism while Mosley made the main plank of his policy opposing the war with Nazi Germany. Mosley ultimately denounced him as a traitor because of his war time activities.

In late August 1939, shortly before war was declared, Joyce and his wife Margaret fled to Germany. Joyce was aware that the British authorities intended to detain him under Defence Regulation 18B. In 1940 he became a naturalised German citizen.

The issue on which the trial of Joyce centred was the passport with which he travelled to Germany. The undisputed facts were that on the 4th July 1933 he applied for a British passport. He obtained it by describing himself as a British subject when he was born and that his birth had

The Trial of William Joyce: Introduction

taken place at Galway Ireland. This was honestly but mistakenly verified by a bank official. Joyce was issued with a passport which was valid for five years. He applied on the 24th September 1938 for a further period of one year and then for yet another period of one year from the 18th July 1939. That was followed by a further application for another extension of a year from the 1st July 1939. That application was dated 24th August 1939 ten days before the outbreak of war.

On 27th August Joyce dissolved his National Socialist League and during the brief period between that date and the outbreak of war in 3rd September 1939 Joyce, together with his recently married second wife Margaret Cairns White, went to Germany. He was granted German nationality in September 1940 and on 12th April 1941 a German military passport was issued to him. On the 26th June he was appointed chief commentator on the German radio for the English group. On the 1st September 1944 came the complete accolade when the *Kriegsverdienstkreuz* was awarded him by The Fuhrer himself.

In November of that year he was issued with a German passport in the name of William Hansen. It is uncertain why the name of Hansen was used, although the turn of the tide against Germany by that time may have caused Joyce to think an alias useful if he fell into the hands of the advancing allies. Oddly his date of birth was given as 11th March 1906 in Galway, Ireland. A month later he was enrolled in the *Volksturm*—the German equivalent of the Home Guard—only this time in his own name, but this time the date and place of his birth were given correctly.

The last broadcast which was identified as coming from Joyce was on 30th April 1945. On 28th May he was arrested by two British officers on the Danish frontier one of whom shot him in the leg.

The British Government was concerned at the start of Joyce's broadcasts that his activities might cause a degree of concern among the people of this country and hence tend to undermine the morale of the population. However this was not to be—in fact the reverse was the case. Joyce became so much a figure of fun that he might almost have been considered working for ourselves against Germany.

However German lack of a sense of humour was unlikely to see it that way. The jocularity was due in no small part to two things. The

Three Cases that Shook the Law

first was the name of Lord Haw-Haw which has been credited to John Barrington of the *Daily Express* and later of the *Sunday Chronicle*. The second was the voice of Joyce which has never been fully defined. To call it an Oxford accent would not merely be an insult to that ancient and much respected university; it would also be grossly inaccurate. It could best be described as a kind of transatlantic notion of how an educated Englishman speaks.

But in addition to these obstacles to any hope of success was the basic hopelessness of his task. He sought to persuade his hearers of the joys of life under the Nazi regime compared with the miserable state of England. The English people were already well-informed about the injustice and cruelty of that dictatorship and wanted no part of it.

The best antidote to this kind of propaganda is ridicule, and it is in this spirit that the people of Britain listened to Joyce's broadcasts. However, once the early part of the war, known as the "phoney" war, was over his audience fell away and never revived.

The BBC assessment of Joyce's broadcasts was:

> "Our impression is that Joyce was not remarkable either for accurate foreknowledge or quick information, though it was plain that he had early access to British news services, papers, magazines etc. presumably through monitoring and from neutral services."

Nevertheless, the fact that "Lord Haw Haw" was not taken seriously in no way detracts from the gravity of his crime of treason—if treason it was.

It was inevitable that William Joyce should be compared with Sir Roger Casement in the First World War. Casement had received honours for his work in the British Consular Service. He was an Irish-man born and bred and an Irish patriot. He was strongly in favour of Irish independence and in 1913 he left the service of the British Government and became involved with the Irish Republican movement. He then worked to obtain German support for an Irish rebellion against British rule. In pursuance of this he visited prisoner of war camps in Germany and tried to incite Irish prisoners of war against the country for which they had been fighting. Even among Irishmen he sometime received a hostile reception. In July 1914, Casement travelled to the United States with colleagues to raise money from among the numerous Irish population for the support of the Irish Volunteers. In late July 1914 he helped to organize and finance gun-running from America to Ireland, and on the outbreak of war in August 1914, together with another man, John Devoy, he arranged a meeting in New York with the Western Hemispheres top-ranking German Diplomat Count Bernstoff when he prepared a plan by which Germany would sell guns to the Irish rebels and provide military leaders, while the rebels would stage a revolt against England, diverting troops from the war against Germany. Negotiations were conducted on Casement's behalf with the German Ambassador to Italy and Prince Von Bulow. In October 1914, Casement travelled in disguise to Germany.

In November 1914 he negotiated the following declaration by Germany:

> "The Imperial Government formerly declares that under no circumstances would Germany invade Ireland with a view to its conquest or the overthrown of any native institutions in that country. Should the result of this, that was not of Germany's seeking, ever bringing in its course German troops to the shores of Ireland they would arrive there, 'not as an army of invaders to pillage and destroy but as the forces of a government that is inspired by goodwill towards a country and a people for whom Germany desires only prosperity and national freedom."

Casement, who had hoped to be part of the Easter Rising, was taken by a German submarine to Ireland where he was arrested on 21st April 1916.

He was tried in the King's Bench Division before a court of three judges and a jury, under the old and highly technical procedure in cases of treason. Joyce, by way of contrast, was arrested in 28th May 1945 and was kept on the continent, where he had been in hospital as a result of the wound he had received at the time of his arrest. Parliament then passed the Treason Act of 1945, a statute which was nominally purely procedural, to assimilate the procedure for any form of treason in all respects to that on a trial for murder.

The main issue in the Casement trial was whether a person could be convicted of treason in respect of acts committed outside the King's dominions. The case definitely settled the law on that point and it was no longer open to Joyce's counsel.

In the trial of Joyce the crucial questions of law (as it then stood) were:

1. Does any British court have jurisdiction to try an alien for a crime committed abroad (other than piracy)?
2. If there was such jurisdiction to try him, did the fact that Joyce had applied for and obtained a British passport impose on him a duty of allegiance during its currency, even when he was outside the British Dominions?

The question to which this second matter gave rise was: what are the conditions in which an alien may owe allegiance to the British Crown and when and how may such a temporary or local allegiance conclude?

There was no issue on the facts regarding Joyce's actions. The question was one of law, which made the task of the courts even more difficult from the point of view of public opinion. For such an unpopular figure to escape the consequences of his treachery on a point of law could cause a riot.

The Treason Act 1945 received the Royal assent on 15th June 1945. Joyce was charged at Bow Street Magistrates' Court on the 18th June before the chief magistrate, Sir Bertrand Watson as follows:

> "William Joyce is charged for that he in the county of London within the Metropolitan Police District and within the jurisdiction of the Central Criminal Court committed high treason between the 22nd day of September 1939 and the 29th day of May 1945, in that he, being a person owing allegiance to His Majesty the King adhered to the King's enemies elsewhere other than in the King's realm, to wit, in the German realm, contrary to the Treason Act 1351."

Joyce was committee to the Central Criminal Court on 28th June 1945. Mr Derek Curtis-Bennett KC applied for an adjournment so that enquiries could be made regarding the nationality of the defendant. This, he submitted, was an absolutely vital element in the case.

There was a record of the birth of William Joyce in New York in 1906 and it would be the submission of the defence that if Joyce was born in the United States he could not owe allegiance to the British Crown.

At the adjourned hearing Joyce faced three charges. The first two were amended to include the words "being a British National", but since Mr Justice Tucker considered that the evidence that Joyce was an American citizen was clear the Attorney-General agreed to accept a plea of not guilty on those counts and proceeded only on the third count which alleged that Joyce, being a person owing allegiance to our Lord the King, adhered to the King's enemies elsewhere than in the realm by broadcasting between 18th September 1939 and 2nd July 1940. (Joyce's British passport expired on this latter date).

Mr Justice Tucker ruled as a matter of law that Joyce did owe allegiance to the British Crown. There could be no issue on the facts, and consequently Joyce was convicted.

The defence gave notice of appeal to the Court of Criminal Appeal against conviction on four grounds:

1. The [trial] court wrongly assumed jurisdiction to try an alien for an offence against British law committed in a foreign country.
2. The learned judge was wrong in law in holding, and misdirected the jury in directing them that the appellant owed allegiance to His Majesty the King during the period from 18th September 1939 to 2nd July 1940.
3. There was no evidence that the renewal of the appellant's passport afforded him or was capable of affording him any protection or that the appellant ever availed himself or had any intention of availing himself of any such protection.
4. If, (contrary to the appellants contention) there was any such evidence, the issue was one for the jury and the learned judge failed to direct them thereon.

We shall consider each of these points as they were argued at the trial.

Before starting our study of the trial of Joyce it may be appropriate to consider the character and mental processes of this strange man who had spent the war years in a hopeless quest to undermine the morale of the British people with a series of broadcasts which competed with programmes such as "ITMA" (It's That Man Again) and "Hi Gang" for laughter. Perhaps one can do that most effectively by reading a statement which he dictated to an intelligence officer while he was in the prison hospital pending his trial:

> "I take this opportunity of making a preliminary statement concerning the motives which led me to come to Germany and to broadcast to Britain over the German radio service. I was actuated not by the desire for personal gain, material or otherwise, but solely by political conviction. I was brought up as an extreme conservative, with strong imperialistic ideas, but very early in my career namely in 1923, I became attracted to Fascism and subsequently to National Socialism. Between the years of 1923 and 1939 I pursued vigorous political activities in England, at times as a Conservative, but mainly as a Fascist or National Socialist. In the period immediately before this war I was profoundly discontented with the policies pursued by British governments, first because I felt they would lead to the eventual disruption of the British Empire, and secondly because I thought the existing economic system entirely inadequate to the needs of the times. I was greatly impressed by the construction work which Hitler had done for Germany and was of the opinion that throughout Europe and also in Britain there must come a reform on the lines of National Socialist doctrine, although I did not suppose that every aspect of National Socialism as advocated by Germany would be accepted by the British People.
>
> One of my dominant beliefs was that a war between Britain and Germany would be a tragedy, the effects of which Britain and the British Empire would not survive, and I considered that a grossly disproportionate influence was exercised on British policy by the Jews, who had their reasons for hating National Socialist Germany.

When in August 1939 the final crisis emerged, I felt that the question of Danzig afforded no just cause for a world war, as by reason of my opinions. I was not conscientiously disposed to fight for Britain against Germany, I decided to leave the country since I did not wish to play the part of a conscious objector, and since I supposed that in Germany I should have the opportunity to express and propagate views the expression of which would be forbidden in Britain during time of war. Realising, however that at this critical juncture I had declined to serve Britain, I drew the logical conclusion that I should have no moral right to return to that country of my own free will and that it would be better for me to apply for German citizenship and make my permanent home in Germany. Nevertheless, it remained my undeviating purpose to attempt as best I could to bring about reconciliation or at least an understanding between the two countries. After Russia and the United Stated had entered the war such an agreement appeared to me no less desirable than before for, although it seemed probably that with these powerful allies Britain would succeed in defeating Germany, I considered that the price which would ultimately have to be paid for this help would be far higher than the price involved in a settlement with Germany.

This belief was strengthened from month to month as the power of Russia grew, and during the later stages of the war I became certain that Britain, even though capable of gaining a military triumph over the Germans would in the end be confronted with a situation far more dangerous and complicated than that which existed in August 1939; and thus until the very last moment I clung to my hope of an Anglo-German understanding, although I could see that the prospects there were very small. I know that I have been denounced as a traitor and I resent the accusation as I conceive myself to have been guilty of no underhand or deceitful act against Britain, although I am also able to understand the resentment that my broadcasts have in many quarters aroused. Whatever opinion may be formed at the present time with regard to my conduct, I submit that the final judgement cannot be properly passed until it is seen whether Britain can win the peace. Finally I should like to stress the fact that in coming to Germany and in working for the German radio system my wife was powerfully influenced by me. She protests to the contrary, but I am sure if I had not taken this step she would not have taken it either.

This statement has been read over to me and it is true."

(Signed) William Joyce

CHAPTER 12

The Indictment

1. First Count

Statement of Offence

High Treason, by adhering to the King's enemies elsewhere other than the King's realm, to wit in the German realm, contrary to the Treason Act, 1351

Particulars of Offence

William Joyce, on the 18th day of September 1939, and on diverse other days thereafter, and between that day and the 29th day of May 1945, being then to wit, on the said several days a person owing allegiance to our lord the King and whilst on the said several days an open and public war was being prosecuted and carried on by the German Realm and its subjects against our lord the King and his subjects, then, and on the said several days traitorously contriving and intending to aid and assist the said enemies of our Lord the King against our Lord the King and his subjects did traitorously adhere to and aid and comfort the said enemies in parts beyond the seas without the realm of England to wit in the realm of Germany, by broadcasting to the subjects of our Lord the King propaganda on behalf of the said enemies of our lord the King.

2. Second Count

Statement of Offence
High Treason, by adhering to the King's enemies elsewhere than in the King's realm, to wit, in the German realm, contrary to the Treason Act 1351.

Particulars of Offence
William Joyce, on the 26th day of September 1940, being then a person owing allegiance to our Lord the King, and while on the said day an open and public war was being prosecuted and carried on by the German Realm and its subjects against our Lord the King and his subjects, then traitorously contriving and intending to aid an assist the said enemies of our Lord the Kings against our Lord the King and his subjects did traitorously adhere to and aid and comfort the said enemies in parts beyond the seas without the realm of England, to wit, the Realm of Germany, by purporting to become naturalised as a subject of the realm of Germany.

3. Third Count

Statement of Offence
High Treason by adhering to the King's enemies elsewhere than in the King's realm, to wit, in the German Realm, contrary to the Treason Act 1351.

Particulars of Offence
William Joyce, on the 18th day of September 1939, and on diverse other days thereafter and between that day and the 2nd July 1940, being then, to wit, on the said several days, a person owing allegiance to our Lord the King and whilst on the said several days an open and public war was being presented and carried on by the German realm and its subjects against our Lord the King and his subjects, then, and on the said several days traitorously contriving and intending to aid and assist the said enemies of our Lord the King against our Lord the King and his subjects did traitorously adhere to and aid and comfort the said enemies in parts

beyond the seas without the realm of England, to wit, in the realm of Germany by broadcasting to the subjects of our Lord the King propaganda on behalf of the said enemies of our Lord the King.

On the third day of the trial the indictment was amended by substituting the words "British subject" in counts one and two, thereby making clearer the distinction between those counts in which the prosecution based their case on British nationality and the third count in which they relied on the obtaining of a British passport as importing the duty of allegiance. On this basis the defendant's plea of not guilty to counts one and two was accepted.

In her well researched book *The Meaning of Treason* Rebecca West points out that Joyce always thought of himself as British. His American birth clearly meant nothing to him. In that sense he might be said to owe a form of allegiance to the Crown, although not one which had ever formed per the 17th-century Hale's *History of the Pleas of the Crown*.

> "Because the subject hath his protection from the King and his laws, so on the other side the subject is bound by his allegiance to be true and faithful to the King. And hence it is that if an alien enemy came into this kingdom hostilely to invade it, if he be taken he shall be dealt with as an enemy, but not as a traitor, because he violates no trust or allegiance. But if an alien, the subject of a foreign prince in amity with the King, live here, and enjoy the benefits of the King's protection, and commit a treason, he shall be judged and executed as a traitor, for he owes a local allegiance."

West continues:

> "There could be no doubt whatsoever that William Joyce owed that kind of allegiance. He had certainly enjoyed the protection of the English Law for some thirty years preceding his departure to Germany. The lawyers for the defence, in proving that he did not owe the natural kind of allegiance which springs from British birth, had found themselves under the necessity of disproving beyond all doubt that he owed this other acquired kind; and there were the two damning sentences in his statement: 'We were generally

counted as British subjects during our stay in Ireland and England…We were always treated as British during the period of my stay in England whether we were or not.' Thus, although an alien, William Joyce owed the Crown allegiance and was capable of committing treason against it. Again he was heading for conviction. But not for certain. There was a definition of the law which was likely to help him."

West explains how in 1907 an assembly of judges laid it down that: "If such an alien seeking the protection of the Crown having a family and effect here should during a war with his native country go thither and there adhere to the King's enemies for the purpose of hostility, he might be dealt with as a traitor. For he came and settled here under the protection of the Crown. And though his person was removed for a time, his effects and family continued still under the same protection." She then continues:

"Now the letter of this judgement did not apply to William Joyce. He had taken his wife with him to Germany, and by that marriage he was childless. He had two children by a former marriage, but they were in the care of their mother and did not enter into this case. The effects he possessed when he quitted England were of such a trifling nature that it would be fairer to regard them as abandoned rather than left under the protection of the Crown. Had he retained any substantial property in the country he would not have had to avail himself of the provisions of the Poor Prisoners Defence Act. But he was within the sphere of the spirit of the judgement. Joyce disappeared from England at some time between 29th August 1939, when he was issued an order dissolving the National Socialist League, the Fascist organization of which he was the head, and the 18th September when he entered the service of the German radio. He was the holder of a British passport, it was part of his life-long masquerade as a British subject. He had declared on the application papers that he had been born in Galway, and had not lost the status of a British subject thus acquired."

West explains how Joyce obtained this passport on 6th July 1933 and that there is maybe some significance in that date. He had become a member

The Indictment

of the British Fascists in 1923, when he was 17-years-of-age, but left this organization to become a member of the Conservative party. In January 1933 Hitler seized power in Germany, and later that year Mosley formed the British Union of Fascists, which Joyce joined. This passport was, like all British passports, valid for five years. In July 1938 he let it lapse, but applied on 24th September 1938 for a renewal for one year; and there is, perhaps, some significance in that date also, as the Munich agreement was signed on 29th September.

The next year Joyce was careful not to let it lapse. He applied for renewal over a month before its expiry on 24th August 1939, and there was significance in that date, as the Second-World-War broke out on 3rd September. Each renewal was dated as if the application had been made when the passport expired. So that when Joyce went to Germany he was the holder of a British passport valid until the beginning of July 1940. This is why the third count of an indictment charged him "with committing high treason by broadcasting between the 18th September 1939 and on diverse other days thereafter, and between that day and the second day of July 1940 being then to wit, on the said several days, a person owing allegiance to our Lord the King." It was the prosecution's case that a person obtaining a passport placed himself or herself thereby under the protection of the Crown and owed it allegiance and that this continued until the passport expired. As West states:

> "No ruling on the point existed, because no case of treason involving temporary allegiance had been tried during the comparatively recent period when passports in their modern sense have been in use, so the judge had to make a new ruling."

It can be noted from the above that references to passports are made in the implied assumption that the passport concerned is a valid one. But not every passport in use is a valid one. Not every passport in use is genuine. Internationally active criminals use forged passports to facilitate the movement of money or other objects of value from one country to another. In the case of the allegedly British passport carried by Joyce on the dates charged that document was falsely obtained and therefore falsely described the nationality of its carrier. The principle of holding a passport when visiting another country was recognised as being protection on the one hand and allegiance on the other. The two things are complimentary. They are reciprocal. But reciprocity must mean a division of responsibility between the two sides. The holder enjoys the right of protection in return for which he gives his allegiance to the protector. But what is the position if the passport has a defect so serious that it nullifies its validity. Is the donor obliged to give that protection if called upon to do so? If the possessor has no legal right to rely upon a bogus document for the means of his protection it must surely follow that the government which issued that same document is released from its duty of protection. The contract is broken on both sides.

There is no right of protection, and hence no duty of allegiance. We shall see how this crucial issue was dealt with by both the prosecution and the defence in the ensuing trial.

CHAPTER 13

The Opening Speech for the Crown

The prosecution case was opened by the newly appointed Attorney-General Sir Hartley Shawcross KC MP. Shawcross was one of the intake of the Labour Government at the time of the landslide victory of the Labour Party in 1945. He was a man of striking good looks and a first-class brain. His rapid rise to high office was inevitable. His style of advocacy was quiet and precise and always courteous and persuasive. However his star quality at the Bar was not equalled by his performance in the hurly burly of party controversy in the House of Commons. It is said that one careless phrase during a debate should have been associated with his career. During a heated exchange he said to the Opposition, "We are the masters now!" Churchill's response was to emphasise that should the electorate, at some future date, return his party to power it would be their pleasure to say, "We are your servants now. However lawyer-politicians frequently excel in one sphere but not the other.

The Attorney-General began his speech to the jury by reminding them that their decision must be made on the basis of the evidence alone, and for this purpose they must put aside personal feelings of animosity towards the defendant. He further dealt with the burden of proof of the prosecution and the division of responsibility between the judge and the jury as to matters of fact and the interpretation of the law.

Sir Hartley Shawcross then outlined the case for the prosecution:

"There are a number of varieties of treason known to our law, all of them striking in a greater or lesser degree at the safety and security of the state, but the treason which is charged against this prisoner in each of the three counts is perhaps the most serious of them all, the treason of giving aid and comfort to the King's enemies, to use the old language of our law which has come down to us for 600 years—the treason of adhering to the King's enemies; the treason of assisting Germany in her war against our country and our King."

The Attorney-General then came to the essence of the crime alleged against Joyce:

"Only those can be convicted of treason who owe a duty of loyalty and faithfulness to the British Crown, only those can be convicted of treason who, in the language of our law, the language that you have heard read in this judgement, owe a duty of allegiance to the Crown, and the first thing that you must have prominently before your minds throughout the whole course of this case is, did this prisoner owe a duty of allegiance to the British Crown?

The very basis of allegiance is this—and I am using now the language of Blackstone, one of the old masters of English law—that as long as the prince affords protection to his subject, so long that subject owes a debt of allegiance to the prince. Protection by the prince, by the Crown, by the state. Protection on one hand, and allegiance on the other hand are, in the submission of the Crown, reciprocal things; correlative things, the two go together. 'Protection'—and again I am using the words of one of our great judges of olden times—'protection draws allegiance just as allegiance draws protection'."

The Attorney-General then turned to the situation regarding aliens:

"That is the common case (native birth) such as most of us find ourselves in, but although that is the ordinary case, and the common case it is not the only case, and from the most ancient times our law has recognised that aliens, people of foreign birth and foreign nationality may place themselves under the protection of the Crown, and that whilst they remain under that protection they may owe and do owe a duty of allegiance to the Crown. In the past it was rarely possible for the Crown to extend that protection beyond our own dominions beyond the Crown's own realm, and so that allegiance which was due from a foreigner was then called local allegiance, because it existed only so long as the alien remained within the locality over which the Crown had jurisdiction; beyond the locality the Crown had no power of exercising protection, but in more modern times owing to the growth of international law, the growth of diplomatic usage, the Crown is able in some respects to extend its protection to subjects beyond the seas. in whatever countries they may go to, and it is the case here for the Crown that whatever his nationality, whether he was British, or whether he was not British, this prisoner is a man who had claimed and asserted the right to British citizenship, who had received the protection which is accorded by the Crown to British citizens, and who had clothed himself in the full status of a British subject, and who in consequence owed a duty of allegiance to the Crown."

Hartley Shawcross then anticipated the defence that the defendant was an American citizen who owed no duty of allegiance to the Crown in the circumstances of this case:

"If that is true — and this is a matter about which you will have to make up your minds when you have heard the whole of the evidence in this case — it would mean that at all times material to this case the prisoner was an American citizen owing no natural duty of allegiance to the British Crown, but was still capable as an alien of placing himself under the protection of the Crown, clothing himself with the status of a British subject and thereby acquiring and taking upon himself an obligation to be loyal and faithful to the British Crown."

Sir Hartley Shawcross then gave a number of examples in which Joyce had claimed to have British citizenship in support of the contention of the prosecution that hereby the defendant received the degree of protection which required allegiance in return. Then he turned to the matter of the passport:

"In a foreign country, friendly, neutral or belligerent, that passport entitled this man to be accorded all the rights and all the protection due to a British subject, nor were those rights insignificant even in Germany even in time of war. In Germany in time of war William Joyce, as the holder of this British passport, was entitled to all those rights which by international law one belligerent power owes to the subjects of another. Those rights Germany could disregard only at her peril, at the peril of reprisals being taken against German subjects held in this country, at the peril of satisfaction being demanded for any wrongs that might have been done to William Joyce, at the end of the war, and in the meantime, possessed of those rights, he enjoyed the full protection which the neutral power looking after British interests in Germany in time of war was able to afford him. He would have been entitled, had he so desired, to call upon that neutral power for whatever assistance or protection he might have required. The Crown say that in these circumstances he had not merely clothed himself with the status of a British subject, he had, so to speak enveloped himself in the Union Jack, secured for himself the greatest protection that he could secure. You may think it small wonder that in these circumstances the prosecution here say that he was required to comport and demean himself as a loyal British subject owing allegiance to the British Crown."

The prosecution called evidence which related to the passports applied for and held by the defendant. Detective Inspector Hunt of the Special Branch at New Scotland Yard gave evidence in which he identified the voice of Joyce broadcasting from Germany during the period stated in the third count when the passport held by Joyce was in force. Although challenged by Mr Gerald O Slade for the defence, the where and when of the broadcasts tended to lose its significance in that Joyce, after arrest, made a written statement in which he admitted his activities on behalf of Germany.

Mr Slade then made a submission that there was no case to go to the jury on any of the three counts in the indictment.

Counts one and two of the indictment had been amended to allege that Joyce was a British citizen.

CHAPTER 14

Submission by the Defence on Counts One and Two

Mr Slade attacked the Crown case on the first two counts on the basis that the doctrine of local allegiance could not possibly nullify the fact that the defendant was not a British subject. If that fact was proved no amount of claims to the contrary by Joyce could alter the well-established principle of English law that birth outside the King's realm meant that such a person was an alien and not a British citizen:

> "With regard to the Counts 1 and 2 I am now submitting to your lordships that there is not even question of status and status must be in every case a question of mixed fact and laws, so far as the country's nationality is concerned, it being of course, a question of English law. My submission to your lordship really comes to this, that I am a Chinese, by screaming from the house tops fifty thousand times that I am a British subject, I do not become one, and secondly, by making fifty thousand declarations that I am a British subject I do not become one; thirdly by swearing an oath that I am a British subject or by a statutory declaration I do not become one, and it makes no difference whether I make these statements because I honestly believed them to be true or whether I make them for some ulterior motive of obtaining a British passport. I cannot alter my status nor can I make a status by anything which I can do. In other words it takes two people at least to make status, the person who is the subject and the Crown in this country who by Act of Parliament or otherwise at common law, confers that status upon that person.

So far as that (the third count) is concerned I respectfully submit it can only be a pure question of law as to which there can be no question at all for the jury. Putting it in its baldest possible form it means this, that a person bot being a British subject, that is to say an alien, can in certain circumstances owe allegiance to His Majesty the King while he is outside His Majesty's dominions. In my respectful submission there is no authority for that statement of the law anywhere."

The case was both shortened and clarified when Mr Justice Tucker said:

"Mr attorney, perhaps you would assist me now by saying whether, having heard the evidence which has been advised by the defence, you are going to invite the jury to come to the conclusion that this man was a British subject or not."

Sir Hartley Shawcross (Attorney-General): No my lord I indicated as far as I properly could in opening that I was not going to press that point and I certainly do not consider it my duty to invite them to say so.

Mr Justice Tucker: Very well, Mr Attorney, I think everybody must agree that the evidence which has been tendered is really overwhelming. That leaves us with 3 counts as the only effective matter which we have to deal with. With regard to that, Mr Attorney, I think it would be perhaps the most convenient course that you should elaborate your submission in regard to that in order that Mr Slade may know how to put his case and then he could reply. At some time I hope you will be able to give me a little assistance in regard to the nature, history and effect of a passport, as to which I am at the moment somewhat ignorant.

CHAPTER 15

The Evidence for the Crown

Let us take another look at count three in the indictment—the only remaining charge facing Joyce and the one around which the battle raged first at the Old Bailey and subsequently in the Court of Criminal Appeal and ultimately in the House of Lords.

Statement of offence

High Treason, by adhering to the King's enemies elsewhere other than in the King's realm, to wit in the German realm, contrary to the Treason Act 1351.

Particulars of offence

William Joyce, on the 18th day of September 1939, and on diverse other days thereafter, and between that day and the 2nd day of July 1940, being then, to wit, on the said several days, a person owing allegiance to our Lord the King, and whilst on the said several days an open and public war was being prosecuted and carried on by the German realm and it's subjects against our Lord the King and his subjects, then, and on the said several days traitorously contriving and intending to aid and assist the said enemies of our Lord the King against our Lord the King and his subjects did traitorously adhere to and aid and comfort the said enemies in parts beyond the seas without the realm of England, to wit in the realm of Germany, by broadcasting to the subjects of our Lord the King propaganda in behalf of the said enemies of our Lord the King.

Never before, in any treason trial, had the duty of allegiance to the Crown been placed on such a tenuous and uncertain basis. The only factual evidence regarding the placing of the broadcasts between the dates of Joyce's departure from England and the expiry of the passport which he possessed was that of Detective Inspector Albert Hunt who testified:

> "I am a Detective Inspector of the Special Branch at New Scotland Yard, I know the prisoner Joyce. I first met him in 1934 when he was a member of the British Union of Fascists, later becoming a member of the National Socialist league. I have not talked to him. During the time he held these positions I listened to public speeches made by him and am thus familiar with his voice. From 3rd September 1939 until 10th December 1939 I was stationed at Folkestone and whilst there remember listening to a broadcast that attracted my attention from what was said in it. I immediately recognized the voice of the person broadcasting as the prisoner's. As far as I can recollect it was about the first month after the outbreak of war, either in September or early October 1939. The prisoner's voice stated that Dover and Folkestone had been destroyed and this remained firmly in my memory on account of the fact that there had been no enemy activity on Folkestone up to that date.
>
> Up to 10th December 1939 I heard him again on the wireless on sundry occasions but took no particular note of what he said. On my return to London on 10th December 1939 I heard his voice on the wireless on a number of occasions between 1940 and 1944."

There was no other live witness to corroborate this evidence.

Nevertheless, the issue around which the crucial conflict lay was the question of allegiance. It was now accepted that Joyce had been born in New York in 1906 and hence was an American citizen. His application for a British passport on 4th July 1933 was therefore invalid, even if by that time he felt himself to be a British citizen rather than an American one.

If the original passport was invalid the same must apply to the passports renewed on 24th September 1938 and the 24th August 1939.

The invalidity remained until the expiry of that passport on 2nd July 1940. Two things were accepted by the court. The first was that Joyce was an American, not a British citizen. The second was that the duty of allegiance is based on the principle of reciprocity. Protection of the passport holder calls for allegiance by that person. Equally allegiance in turn merits the protection. They must coincide. But if the passport is not valid because the person described himself as a British citizen is no such thing does the duty of protection arise? If it does not, then the issuing state is surely entitled to repudiate its obligation to protect if this is called for. Where the passport holder cannot call upon the issuing state to provide protection there can be no corresponding duty of allegiance.

Three Cases that Shook the Law

CHAPTER 16

Crown and Defence Submission on Count Three

It is not my intention to weary the reader by discussing at length the various citations of legal authorities by Sir Hartley Shawcross and Mr Slade. Suffice it to say that while the Attorney-General maintained that the court had jurisdiction to try Joyce, albeit he was an alien and notwithstanding that his treason was committed abroad; Slade for the defence insisted that no such jurisdiction existed and there was no authority to be found in English law which said otherwise.

The Attorney-General set out his case:

> "The passport is an indication that the person, while leaving the country is still remaining tied to the country, and has the intention to return. The form of the application is that it is expressed to be for a 'holiday tour' and there is in the application itself every indication, in my submission, that the passport holder is applying for facilities to leave this country and to go to various countries for a holiday tour with a view to his eventual readmission to this country.
>
> That, perhaps is one of the most important effects of a passport in diplomatic usage. There was at one period a number of people wandering about Europe who found it difficult to find any state which would accept them as its nationals. That was the reason for the present passport system between the two wars. It is clear that the international consequences of the issue of a passport by a state is that the state which issues the passport will readmit the holder to its own territory, and so if the holder goes to Belgium, France, Switzerland, Italy or Austria and they do not want him to stay, they can

deport him with the assurance that the issuing country will receive him back. Without such a passport they might find themselves saddled with an alien whose presence was not wanted and yet find it impossible to deport him to some other country because no other country would receive him.

The passport is not only a certificate of identity, but it is an undertaking that the person who holds it would be allowed to return. I would invite your lordships to say that, as in the case quoted in Foster and East, the alien who leaves his country, but has his family remaining behind him, the presence of his family being some evidence as to his intention eventually to return, constituting a tie between himself and his country, so here the existence of a passport is some evidence of intention to return and is some tie between the alien and the state."

The contention of the Crown was that, on the basis of a resolution of the judges in the 18th-century, Joyce would be guilty as an alien if, as was submitted was the case, when he obtained his British Passport he intended to return to this country. There was not a jot of evidence that Joyce had any such intention. He left with his wife. He did not leave either family or effects.

"Family" in this context must mean wife and children, not parents and others over whom he has no control.

Mr Justice Tucker took the point when he commented:

"Mr Attorney if that is right, that I think would be a question for the jury would it not — the intention with which the passport is taken out and used?"

The Attorney-General who must have realised the point was weak in logic and virtually wholly unsupported by authority agreed with the judge.

The Attorney-General continued to put his case:

"Putting the whole thing in a sentence I would submit on behalf of the Crown, that it is unthinkable that a person who has apparently been domiciled in this country, who has the whole of his family living in this country, and who leaves the whole of his family, his relations, his father and mother his sisters and brothers with the exception of his wife, in this country who has received from this country, who has secured from this country the substantial matter of protection that the issue of a passport involves, who has secured the right to return to this country at any time as a British subject, who has declared himself to be a British subject, who uses the passport and travels on it as a British subject, even perhaps, as in this case, secures employment on it—it is in my submission unthinkable that such a person should not at the corresponding date owe allegiance to the Crown. I would ask your lordship to deal with the matter, and I submit it in this way under two heads that here is a man who was resident and indeed domiciled in this country—all the evidence goes to show that—and who left it for a period of time for a purely temporary purpose retaining the tie of his passport and some family relationships, and, secondly, on the basis that here was a man who quite independently of any continuing residence of that kind was under a duty of allegiance because of the protection of the Crown with which he had clothed himself."

The allegiance alleged by the Attorney-General would be more persuasive but for two considerations. Firstly, there is no evidence that Joyce left England in August 1939 for "A period of time for a purely temporary purpose" and secondly the purpose he left for was a fraudulent one since it wrongly describes its holder as a British citizen.

On behalf of the defence Mr Slade made his submissions. His basic proposition was that it was well established English law that an alien owed no duty of allegiance to the British Crown, in respect of actions committed in a foreign country. "We maintain that all the authorities in statute and case law confirmed this, with one exception only. This arose in *Foster's Crown Law*. Here it was stated 'with regard to natural born subjects there can be no doubt. They owe allegiance to the Crown at all times and in all places. This is what we call natural allegiance, in contra distinction to that which is local. The duty of allegiance whether natural or local is founded on the relation the person standeth to the Crown. And in privileges he deriveth this from that relation. Local allegiance is founded in the protection of a foreigner enjoyed for his person, his family or effects during his residence here; and it ceaseth whenever he withdraweth with his family and effects'. This theory is expounded further with these words : 'And if such alien seeking the prosecution of the Crown having a family and effects here should during a war with his native country' — Joyce left in August 1939 — and did adhere to the King's enemies for purposes of hospitality, thus he might be dealt with as a traitor. He came and settled here under the protection of the Crown and although his person was removed for a time his effects and family continued still under the same protection. This rule was laid down by all the judges assembled at the Queen's command on January 12th 1707". Counsel for the defence quoted further:

> "Local allegiance is that which is due from a foreigner during his residence here, and is founded in the protection he enjoys for his own person, his family and effects during his residence here, and is founded in the protection he enjoys for his own person and his family and effects during the time of that residence. This allegiance ceases whenever he withdraws with his family and effects"

Slade continued:

> "The argument of the Attorney-General for this moment is leaving out the family and the effects, this allegiance ceases whenever he withdraws his family and effects provided he has no *animus revertandi*— those are the words which the Attorney-General is asking your Lordship to read into that for the moment—

> For his temporary protection being then at an end and the duty arising from it also terminates but if he only goes abroad himself, leaving his family and effects here under the same protection the duty still continues; and if he committed treason he may be punished as a traitor and this whether his own sovereign be an enemy or at peace with ours."

Slade dealt with this argument of the prosecution in the following forthright manner:

"I will deal with the question of a passport when I come to it, but may I say that you do not leave your family here when you leave your father here. You have got no say whether your father will stay here or whether he will go elsewhere. You do not leave your family here by leaving your brother, who is of age or anyone else who is *sui juris,* or anyone else over whom you have no control.

'Your family' means in my respectful submission your wife and your children and 'effects' means the effects which belong to you and not the effects which belong to your father or to your sister or to your brother. The evidence, your Lordship will remember, with regard to the wife—there is no evidence that there are any children—appears, among other places in the prisoner's statement Exhibit 12."

Mr Justice Tucker:

"It is merely a matter of indicating that the severance from this country must be a final act and not something merely temporary."

Slade:

"I submit to your Lordship it means this, that so long as you leave your wife and your family and your effects under the King's protection, that is to say you rely upon the King to protect those who are nearest and dearest to you, and your own effects by being given the help of the law to protect these effects. You cannot say 'I will go off and commit treason somewhere else, leaving my wife and children over here under the protection of His Majesty.' Clearly there was no question of Joyce owing allegiance to the Crown under the above principle, however elegantly argued by the Attorney-General."

Slade then came to the issue of the passport carried by Joyce when he left England:

"We are concerned here with a British passport which had in fact been issued to an American subject. The Crown has no jurisdiction to issue

Three Cases that Shook the Law

British passports to American subjects. Your lordship was told at some stage of this case yesterday the sort of protection that a man owning a British passport became entitled to. Let us see by taking an illustration what sort of protection he would get when ex-hypothesi he is an American subject. Say he goes to Spain and someone in Spain wants to do him an injury and he says 'You may not do that to me. I shall go and see our Ambassador in Madrid', all the time ex-hypothesi being an American having obtained a British passport. He goes to the Ambassador and says 'protect me; this man wants to harm me'. The Ambassador says 'You must not harm this man, he is a British subject'. To which the Spaniard replies 'That is what he tells you. He is an American and your Crown has no right to issue a passport to an American subject', (nor has it any duty to protect an American), I can only ask the question rhetorically, what protection does your lordship think that an American would get in these circumstances in Spain?"

Slade continued:

"Take one more illustration ex-hypothesi as I say Joyce is now an American subject. Supposing in August 1939, when he left Great Britain, instead of going to Germany he had gone to New York, his own country, and supposing America had come into the war against us instead of on our own side, he would have been liable for service in the American army. Whatever he tried to do, if the passport had lasted for a year and it might have lasted for five years — it had an extension for five years — he would commit treason against this country by fighting for his own country."

Mr Justice Tucker:

"I do not want to say anything which would embarrass you at this stage, but when we are dealing with this kind of subject, when you talk of coming back to the country and putting his head in a noose, it might depend on whether we won the war or not, or whether there had been an early peace. All kinds of things may have been in the minds of people in August 1939."

Slade replied with a significant point:

"I respectfully agree. He would only come back if there were an early peace which resulted in a victory for Germany. I merely cite the words 'The King cannot authorise wrong'—His Majesty the King would not dream of authorising the issue of a British passport to an American citizen. The only reason it was done in this case was because the Foreign Office was deceived by the mis-statement made in the form of application."

Mr Slade pointed out, and the judge agreed that there was nothing in the Treason Act of 1351 that dealt with the position where an alien committed an offence in another country. Or in any other Act of Parliament for that matter:

"I am merely saying that it would be quite inconsistent with the ordinary comity of nations for one nation to arrogate to itself the right to try subjects of another nation for acts committed while they were in the territory of that nation. If that were not so, anyone, to take a fantastic case, could take an American subject who was paying a visit over here and try him over here for a murder which it was alleged he had committed in New York. There was every reason for the rule laid down by the learned Chief Justice, because that is exactly what one would expect when dealing with the question of whether the statute applies to British subjects generally or only to British subjects within the United Kingdom or the Dominions. He then says even if that construction is possible or even probable you must extend it to aliens abroad, because that would be contrary to international comity."

Further Submission by the Prosecution

Let us see how the Attorney-General dealt with the submissions of the defence and how valid they appear on further reflection:

"My Lord, may I first of all deal with the point of jurisdiction. In my submission that point really begs the whole question in this case, the question whether or not the person was under a duty of allegiance to the Crown. If one looks at the statute, and in my submission it cannot be doubted that it is within the power of Parliament to pass a statute creating criminal offences by foreigners abroad; if one looks at the original statute of treason, it is clear on that statute as construed in the *Casement Case* (1917) 1KB 98 that it does apply to offences committed outside the realm. That was of course the great argument in the Casement Case, as your lordship will remember. It was contended in that case, although no question of nationality arose, that the statute was limited to offences committed within the realm, and after considerable argument in the trial, it was held that it applied to offences wherever they were committed.

The statute itself, as to the persons who might commit the offence of treason, appears to cover anybody, British subjects or foreigners, any person. The effect of the cases has been to qualify the statute to this extent, that it only covers those persons who are under a duty of allegiance to the Crown. One is then thrown back to what is, in my submission, one of the primary questions in this case: Was the prisoner under a duty of allegiance to the Crown?"

It is as well, first of all, to recognise that the Casement case bears little or no comparison with that of Joyce. It was not contested that Casement was a British citizen whereas that was the whole issue in Joyce's case. He was not.

The attorney-general then argued that the English court had jurisdiction to try the case before it because,

"I think it right to say that there is hardly a state in the world which does not, in fact, exercise a protective jurisdiction over foreigners in respect of crimes committed outside its own territory."

All the Attorney-General is saying, at considerable length, is that if Joyce was a person owing allegiance to the Crown the court has jurisdiction to try him — but did such allegiance exist? The prosecution has based its case on allegiance fairly and squarely on the passports carried by Joyce when he defected. As to the matter of the passport the Attorney-General had this to say:

"If there is no precedent for this case it is simply because in no previous case have comparable circumstances arisen. Now the passport is a document of comparatively modern growth. There have been very few cases—there has been one certainly of treason since the introduction of passports: indeed passports only came into general use in the course of this century and in the course of that time there has, as far as I can recall, been one case, and one only, under the Treason Act. Foster and East, are in my submission powerful authorities for the view that the essential basis of allegiance is the right to protection, especially when one remembers there is excluded from the obligation of allegiance the possibly resident but non protected alien."

A key phrase employed by the Attorney-General was, "Once the protection arises it continues until by some positive act of election on the part of the Crown it is withdrawn."

Be that as it may, the real issue is; when does it arise? And does it arise in the case of an American citizen fraudulently obtaining a British passport by false statements as to his nationality in order to leave the realm to commit traitorous offences for a foreign power? This is the crux of the issue.

The judge was quick to take this point. The discussion in court now centred round the passport which Joyce was carrying. The Attorney-General used these somewhat surprising words:

"I am relying on his own statement and on the fact that he had a German passport. There is no authority whatever for the proposition that the Crown has no jurisdiction to issue a passport to an American subject and in my submission it is clearly wrong. It is, done, I will not say every day, but with considerable frequency."

Following this assertion, the judge quickly pointed out the fallacy of this statement as it stood:

"I have no evidence about it, Mr Attorney. As far as my researches show passports, I understand are issued as part of the prerogative of the Crown, and I suppose that under that prerogative the Crown issues a passport to whomsoever it likes, but of course it is unthinkable that the Crown would issue a British passport to an American citizen describing himself as a British citizen."

This is the absolute crux of the matter and the Attorney-General's somewhat lame reply relates to dual passports which are completely irrelevant to the case before the court:

"In practice that would undoubtedly be the position but not always, because the position of dual nationality is well recognised and it is particularly recognised in the case of America. There is no evidence of this, but it is, I think a matter of law. An American woman who marries a British subject acquires British nationality and is thereby entitled to an American passport because she does not lose her American nationality."

This illustration is completely beside the point. Such a woman has acquired British nationality, which Joyce never did; Mr Justice Tucker pointed this out: "She gets a British passport as a British subject by international law." To this the Attorney-General replied with a proposition which appears to strain the principle of law regarding allegiance to the Crown to the uttermost:

"Yes, My Lord, but the sole fact that a person has another status is no reason why the British Crown cannot grant a British passport. If my friend had put it on the other basis, that the Crown had no jurisdiction to grant a British passport to a person who is not a British subject, then, if I may say so with respect, he might have been on a little stronger ground, but even so my submission is that it is quite clear that such a submission would have been wrong, indeed the very application form which is in evidence in this case refers not only to British subjects and to naturalized subjects but to British protected subjects, and a British passport can be issued and is issued to persons whether they be British subjects or not whom the Crown in the exercise of its prerogative powers thinks it right to protect."

Crown and Defence Submission on Count Three

The crucial words here are, "Whom the Crown in the exercise of its prerogative thinks it right to protect."

The Crown has discretion, but surely that assertion can only be properly exercised on correct information as to the status of the applicant for the passport. If the information is false and the passport has been obtained by false pretences could the Crown be held to its duty of protection? If it could not, then would the corresponding duty of allegiance arise? If this were not the case then every criminal who held a British passport validly issued, though under false pretences, would be entitled to the Crown's protection in whatever part of the world he happened to be when carrying out his criminal activities.

Dealing with another situation the Attorney-General said this:

> "My Lord, I think I would with respect, be inclined to put it on the two feet: one of residence, defining residence at the lowest in this sense, as continuing until the ties which made the resident a subject of this country had been broken, and one of the ties would be the existence of a passport. If the resident alien leaves the country he leaves it with a passport, enabling him to return to the country, he leaves it with a passport which is issued to him for the purpose of going on holiday, then he continues to be resident for the purpose of the authorities. Alternatively, if not resident in that sense, he continues to be protected by the possession of the passport."

But surely the principle can only apply when the passport has been validly issued—that is to say to an alien, not to an alien posing as a British subject.

It was then, however, that the judge dropped his bombshell:

> "Mr Attorney and Mr Slade, I shall direct the jury on count three that on the 24th August 1939, when the passport was applied for the prisoner beyond a shadow of a doubt owed allegiance to the Crown of this country, and that on the evidence given, if they accept it, nothing happened at the material time thereafter to put an end to the allegiance that he then owed. It will remain for the jury, and for the jury alone, as to whether or not at

the relevant dates he adhered to the King's enemies. If both or either of you desire to address the jury on that issue of course now is your opportunity."

The judge had now ruled against the defence on the issue of law as to whether Joyce owed allegiance — the ruling was that he did. The only remaining question of fact was did anything happen to disqualify that allegiance. Slade had very little chance in the face of Inspector Hunt's evidence. Slade did his best, but he was very much on the back foot:

"The only question is he [Hunt] mistaken, or as I would rather put it, are you satisfied beyond reasonable doubt that he could not be mistaken? These are the points which I would ask you to bear in mind. You have heard the language that Joyce used in 1943 and 1944. It has all been given in evidence. However, you may disagree with it, or however you may have been amused by it, at any rate it is a reasoned statement — it is not the sort of statement which you would describe, and that I would describe as the grotesque statement, that in September 1939, or maybe up to 3rd October 1939, Folkestone and Dover had been destroyed. There were no visits of aeroplanes to this country at that time, there were no atomic bombs; there was nothing whatsoever to destroy Folkestone or Dover. There were no long distance guns capable of coming from Germany to this country. The French coast was still in the hands of the French. It would have been a fantastic thing to say."

The Attorney-General's closing speech dealt a devastating blow to this point made by the defence:

"You are asked to discredit and reject the evidence of Inspector Hunt in regard to the actual terms of the broadcast which he heard at the end of September or early in October to the effect that Dover and Folkestone had been destroyed, and you are asked to say that you are not satisfied that that broadcast was made because the making of it would have been a fantastic thing. Members of the jury, fantastic no doubt to people living in Dover or Folkestone, fantastic it may be to people living in this country at that time and knowing exactly how the war was progressing, but not quite so fantastic, do you think to British soldiers, if you will, in the far flung outposts of the empire, to British garrisons abroad, and not only to British soldiers, but English people in foreign parts able to listen to the wireless propaganda of the Germans, but not able so readily perhaps to get accurate immediate and first-hand knowledge of what was actually happening in England at that time. It would not have been impossible for Germany to destroy Folkestone and Dover as they had destroyed other places in other parts of Europe, and you may think that however fantastic those statements might have appeared to Inspector Hunt in Folkestone, their effect upon listeners in distant parts might have been of a very different kind."

Three Cases that Shook the Law

CHAPTER 17

The Judge's Summing-up

After the usual preliminary observations regarding the burden of proof and the diversion of responsibility between the judge and the jury the judge thought it reasonable and proper to let the members of the jury know why he had ruled as he had on the legal issue:

> "The first thing that the prosecution have got to establish is that at the material time the prisoner William Joyce was a person owing allegiance to our Lord the King. Now, in my view I have already intimated, after hearing the very learned and very helpful submissions that have been made by both the learned counsel in this case; the conclusion that I have reached as a matter of law is, if you, as a jury, accept the facts which have been proved in this case without contradiction—of course you are entitled to believe anything if you wish—if you accept the facts which have been proved and not denied in this case, then at the time in question, as a matter of law, this man, William Joyce, did owe allegiance to our Lord the King, not withstanding the fact that he was not a British subject at the material time."

The learned judge then dealt with the law of treason regarding British subjects before turning to the question of allegiance:

> "There can be no doubt or question that an alien, an alien friend, owes allegiance to the Crown of this country so long as he is resident within the Realm. The question which has arisen in this case is whether or not an alien who has undoubtedly—undoubtedly—put himself under the protection and thereby acquired a status by which he owes allegiance to the Crown

can divest himself of that allegiance by setting foot off the shores of this country, although in doing so he may still be availing himself of the protection which is offered to British subjects by the issue of a passport, what has been picturesquely described by the learned Attorney-General as leaving this country wrapped up in the Union Jack. That is the issue in this case, and the fact that there has never been a case precisely like it is not conclusive one way or another."

Surely, however, the question still remains as to whether the British Crown would be obliged to afford protection to an alien holder of a fraudulently obtained passport, and if not would the alien be entitled to avail himself of that non-obligatory protection? If he would not, is there a duty of allegiance? The judge conceded that:

"You cannot become a British citizen by carrying a British passport. There is no such thing known to our law as crime by estoppel, as it is called. Non the less I think it is the law that if a man who owes allegiance by having made his home here, having come to live here permanently, thereby acquiring allegiance as he undoubtedly does, then steps out of this realm armed with the protection which is normally afforded to a British subject—improperly obtained, maybe, but none the less obtained—if he leaves this realm, as the Attorney—General called it, wrapped up in the Union Jack, that is to say, using and availing himself of the protection of the Crown in an executive capacity which covers him while he is abroad he does not thereby divest himself of the allegiance which he already owes."

The judge described the extensive period which Joyce had lived in England, his various activities and the fact that when applying for the original passport in 1933 he described himself as a British citizen. He applied the principle of "local allegiance" in clear terms:

"It seems to me to indicate that the real basis of this law of treason is founded upon the protection which a man is receiving from the Crown to which he has acquired allegiance by residence, I see no reason whatever why that allegiance and that protection should not cover him while he is away from this country carrying the King's passport just as much as when he has left his ox and his ass behind him in this country."

The judge then turned to the facts of the case, dealing mainly with the evidence of Inspector Hunt. He concluded with these words:

"You have heard the whole of this case. You have had the assistance, if I may say so, of the admirable addresses you have listened to by the learned Attorney-General, who has put the matter so fully before you. You have also had, and I have had, what I agree entirely to have been the distinguished assistance of Mr Slade in this matter. Now members of the jury, Mr Slade may be, for all I know having a very uncongenial task in this case. But how can justice be administered if people charged with these offences are not defended, by able and responsible counsel? How can you not get at the truth of any matter unless members of the Bar, acting in accordance with the highest traditions of the Bar, put their services at the disposal of men of all kinds and of all races, whatever the charge may be that is brought against them? Members of the jury, some people sometimes talk about the law's delays and clamour for what is called swift justice. This case was postponed from the July sessions to the September sessions. Supposing it had not been what would have been the result? Look at this mass of evidence that has been obtained from America and elsewhere with the assistance of those legal gentlemen who have put themselves at the service of this man in order that you, as a British jury, may know the real and true facts before you arrive at your verdict."

The jury retired and after a very short period of time returned with a guilty verdict. Joyce was sentenced to death. There remained an appeal.

Three Cases that Shook the Law

CHAPTER 18

The Appeal

Following the trial there were appeals both to the Court of Criminal Appeal and to the House of Lords. For the defence much the same arguments were advanced as had been placed before the judge at the Old Bailey. Likewise the Attorney-General replied in kind on behalf of the Crown. Each court supported the ruling of Mr Justice Tucker on the law and saw no reason for interfering with the verdict of the jury, save only for Lord Porter who delivered a dissenting judgement in the House of Lords. It would be exhausting for the reader and a pointless exercise to reiterate the arguments put forward, but the following passages from the judgement of the Lord Chief Justice, Lord Hewart embody the view of the Court of Criminal Appeal:

> "The importance of the matter in the decision of the present case is twofold. If the law as stated by Foster is correct, it is clear that Mr Slade has put his case much too high in claiming, as he does, that the appellant could not in law be guilty of high treason committed abroad because he was not a British subject and, secondly, it seems to negative a further proposition based on want of jurisdiction to be referred to later in this judgement. It does not purport to show that the present appellant was guilty of the crime charged since the case put does not apply here, there being no evidence that the appellant on going abroad left his wife and effects behind him. It still remains for the Crown to show that upon the proved facts of this case he did owe the duty of allegiance to his Majesty. If there was no other evidence upon the subject than the proved fact of his departure from England after 24th August the Crown might be in a great difficulty and we express no

opinion as to what would have been the proper course to adapt, beyond observing that it might have been necessary to leave further matters to the jury since the jury alone can draw inferences of fact from such as evidence as they accept. But in our judgement the facts relating to the application for, the granting of, and the renewal of, the passport this case make it clear that as a matter of law the appellant was still owing allegiance to the Crown when he commenced to adhere to the King's enemies by broadcasting as alleged in the indictment and found by the jury."

As to the passport the Lord Chief Justice said:

"The form of passport issued in this case requests the foreign government and requires the diplomatic and consular or representatives of his Majesty to allow the holder to pass freely without let or hindrance and to afford him every assistance and protection of which he may stand in need, and the possession of such a document clearly entitles the holder to return to the country which has issued the passport. It is therefore plainly a protection in every sense of the word to the holder while he is absent from the King's realm. We entertain no doubt that if it is possible for a foreigner to owe the duty of allegiance to the British Crown, although not that the moment within the British realm, as we think it is, the appellant at the time when he adhered to the King's enemies did owe that allegiance."

The proceedings at the House of Lords followed the ruling of the court of criminal appeal. Save for Lord Porter, who, while agreeing with the rest of the House on the matter of allegiance considered the discretion of the judge to be in error regarding the renewal of the passport and hence a substantial miscarriage of justice had occurred.

Joyce was executed on the 3rd January 1946.

CHAPTER 19

Conclusion

Rebecca West, in her brilliant work *The Meaning of Treason* wrote of the sentence of death on Joyce:

"The judge announced that beyond a shadow of doubt William Joyce had owed allegiance to the Crown of this country when he applied for his passport, and that nothing had happened to put an end to that allegiance during the period when that allegiance was valid, in other words, he ruled that a person holding a British passport owed allegiance to the Crown even when he was outside the realm. This ruling made it quite certain that Joyce was going to be sentenced to death. If the sentence were carried out he would die the most completely unnecessary death that any criminal has ever died on the gallows. He was the victim of his own and his father's life—long determination to lie about their nationality. For had he not renewed his British passport, and had he left England for Germany on the American passport which was rightfully his, no power on earth could have touched him. As he became a German citizen by naturalization before America came into the war, he could never have been the subject of prosecution under the American laws of treason."

On the same argument it might be said that had Frederick Bywater's not retained the letters he received from Edith Thompson she would not have been hanged. The real issue in both cases is whether, on the evidence presented to the court, the verdicts and sentence were right.

Many lawyers were uncomfortable with the verdict in the Joyce case. The over-arching fact was that Joyce was an American citizen who had a British passport to which he was not entitled. Could he be said by any unilateral actions of his own to have divested him of his American nationality?

The American law on the subject at the time is irrelevant. Joyce was tried in an English court according to English law. A passport which describes an American as an English man is invalid and defective. Does it provide protection and if not does it create allegiance? The bearer of a cheque which misdescribes the person cannot oblige the bank to honour it, nor is a carrier obliged to accept a ticket which has a similar defect.

The British constitution has a basic principle that Parliament makes the law and the judges apply it. Sometimes judges of the highest courts "make" new law. This remains in force unless and until Parliament rules otherwise. The law as interpreted in the Joyce trial remains in force. Parliament has not seen fit to change or amend it. But the right of the citizen, as layman and lawyer to criticise the decisions of even the judicial committee of the House of Lords (now the Supreme Court of Justice) remains a democratic privilege of this country.

PART 3
TIMOTHY EVANS

Three Cases that Shook the Law

CHAPTER 20

Introduction: The Trial of Timothy Evans

In the long and lamentable history of murder in the United Kingdom there are a few which for horror and brutality occupy a position which will make them unforgettable. Examples of these are the Moors Murders in which Ian Brady and Myra Hindley tortured and killed at least five young people and the slaughter by Frederick and Rosemary West of no fewer and possibly more than ten girls which included some who were their own daughters. Yet another such case is called to mind by an address in London: 10 Rillington Place. It was here, in a house of incredible squalor that eight people, seven women and a child, were strangled to death and their bodies secreted in various parts of the building and garden. Quite apart from the terrible events which occurred there, such evidence as there is discloses sleazy and rundown conditions such as one would not expect to find still existing in the 1950s.

The house, which has long been demolished, with the others in the neighbourhood, has however yet another claim to fame. It was the catalyst of a trial which resulted in the ultimate nightmare for a system of justice which is weighted in favour of defence — the conviction and sentencing to death of a man ultimately cleared of the crime of which he was accused. That man was named Timothy Evans. Evans was charged with and convicted of the murder of his daughter Geraldine. General features of the trial make it unique. Firstly, he was convicted largely on the evidence of John Reginald Halliday Christie, a serial killer who almost certainly committed the crime for which Evans was hanged.

Secondly, Evans confessed to the murder, a confession which he subsequently withdrew. Having regard to his character, personality and mental age the original confession was palpably false. No allegations of improper conduct on the part of the police to put pressure on Evans were made.

Thirdly, both Evans and Christie were inveterate liars and Christie succeeded in presenting himself to the Crown as an honest and reliable witness.

Fourthly, Evans defence counsel, Malcolm Morris QC, laboured under a severe disadvantage. His instructions were to accuse Christie of having committed the murder of which Evans stood charged, but he had no knowledge of those homicides which Christie had already committed.

Fifthly, the judge, who tried the case was in the final stages of illness which may have influenced his conduct of the trial.

Sixthly, after subsequent enquiries into the trial, Evans was granted a posthumous pardon.

The two names which will forever be connected with the horrific events at 10 Rillington Place are those of Evans and Christie. Let us first look at the character and mental condition of Evans.

Timothy John Evans was born in 1924 at Merthyr Vale in South Wales. He was brought up by his mother, his father having deserted her before he was born. At the age of seven an event occurred which may well have affected his life and future conduct. While bathing in the River Taff he sustained an injury to his foot. The cut was wrapped in a dirty cloth and hence became infected. This was a tubercular condition and a number of operations followed. He missed much of his education and was rejected for National Service. He was particularly short, as is apparent from photographs taken close to the time of his trial.

Evans' main employment seems to have been as a van driver. It should be said in fairness to him that he was always in employment and there was no history of criminal convictions, he kept on the right side of the law.

In September 1947 Evans married Beryl Susanna Thorley, a young telephonist who worked at Grosvenor House. It was a surprising match in that she was a pretty, well turned-out girl of some education and familiar with people of culture while he was an illiterate who could not read or write, with a Welsh working-class background. Evans father was a road haulier and, after her husband had deserted her when she was pregnant, his mother, who had never been granted a certificate that her husband

Introduction: The Trial of Timothy Evans

was presumed dead, remarried Mr Penry Probert in 1929, the same year in which she gave birth to her second daughter Maureen.

Timothy was educated at the local school but he was a backward boy who derived little benefit from it. His father moved to London, but due to the trouble with his injured foot the boy spent some time in hospital before returning to Wales to live with his grandmother. After he left school, Evans obtained employment in the mines, but his physical disability made such work impossible and he returned to London for further treatment.

As an adult Evans was a somewhat pitiful figure. As already noted, he was illiterate and was found after a medical examination, to have the mental age of a boy of ten-and-a-half. He was a frequent visitor to local public houses but although he drank a lot of beer was not known as a drunkard or troublemaker. The most notable feature of his character, and one that has great bearing on the subsequent events in his life, is the fact that he was an almost psychopathically persistent liar. His lying was constant and sometimes absurdly grandiose. The psychological explanation for this is easily apparent. His fantasising was an escape from and a remedy for his crushing insignificance.

Failures sometimes compensate for their lack of achievement by retreating into a world of illusion and daydreams. Such individuals live for what they believe they might or should have been. They prefer comfortable illusion to the cold uncomfortable experience of reality. This is most important to bear in mind when we come to the confessions which Evans made to crimes which were committed by another. Evans' description of himself when he said, "I am not very well-educated. I cannot read or write" was therefore a considerable understatement.

Before continuing with the story of Evan's marriage to Beryl we should take a close look at the other man figuring in the ensuing drama: Christie. No two men could have been more different. Evans was primitive, moronic, backward and pathetic but he was no murderer, indeed there was nothing violent in his personality. Christie was a ruthless serial killer. His homicides were not committed for any material gain. The motive was solely sexual satisfaction — sex of the most savage and bestial kind. Yet the people who knew Christie were firmly under the impression that he was a quiet unoffending man with a background which included service for his country in the Army in the First World War and, further, meritorious conduct as a volunteer member of the police force. Most astonishingly of all is the fact that in Evans' trial he was able to convince a jury and court at the Old Bailey that this was his real character.

Christie, as has been the case with other serial killers, came from a respectable family (in Yorkshire). He was one of seven children, his father was a carpet designer, reputedly a severe and austere man, but his mother was a gentle person. He sang in the church choir, became a boy scout and in due course a scout master. In short, there was nothing abnormal in his childhood which could be said to be the root cause of his mental disturbance in later life. However, an incident occurred which had a strange and significant effect on him. His maternal grandfather died and the boy was taken to view the body of the man of whom he had always been in awe. He was eight-years-old at the time and had never seen a dead body before. Death seemed to exercise a strange fascination over him and an unnatural excitement was something he experienced at the realisation that someone who he had once feared now lay cold and helpless.

He won a scholarship to secondary school where he proved to be an intelligent pupil. After school he worked in cinemas and had his first exposure to sex with a girl who was, unlike himself, of some experience. This encounter was not a success and resulted in a degree of mockery from his friends who called him, "Can't-make-it Christie." This would have proved humiliating for a young man and may have had a far reaching effect on his outlook towards women.

In September 1916, with the First World War under way, Christie enlisted in the Army and at the age of 17 he was called up for service. In March 1918 he was injured by a mustard gas shell and was blinded for some months. His voice also appears to have suffered for a time. Christie was invalided out of the Army in 1919. He was employed in a cinema and then with a wool manufacturer, but he could not settle down to any steady employment. In May 1920 he married Ethel Simpson Waddington. Bride and bridegroom were each aged 22. There were no children of the marriage, which Christie claimed to be for him a disappointment.

Introduction: The Trial of Timothy Evans

Ethel was a jolly Yorkshire woman who, as events proved, made a grave mistake in marrying the psychopathic Christie.

In 1920 Christie began what proved to be the start a criminal record. He had obtained work as a temporary postman and exploited the job by stealing a quantity of postal orders, for which he was sentenced to three months' imprisonment. In January 1923 he was bound over for obtaining money by false pretences and also placed on probation for 12 months for an offence of violence. He came to London, Ethel remaining in Sheffield where she worked as a shorthand typist. In 1924 Christie was sentenced to nine months hard labour for stealing money and goods, and five years later for assaulting with a cricket bat a woman with whom he was living when he received six months' imprisonment with hard labour. Finally, he was sentenced to three months' imprisonment with hard labour and fined for theft of a car. The wide gap in time between these crimes and the subsequent trial for murders in 1953 is a matter of speculation. So strange is the personality of Christie that it will remain a puzzle. And another mystery is why his wife Ethel, after nine years' separation, should decide to resume living with her husband. It proved to be a fatal decision.

In 1938 the Christies took up the occupancy of the ground floor flat at 10 Rillington Place. It consisted of three small rooms. The following year Christie took a step which did much to enable him to pose as a commendable Englishman at the trial of Evans in 1950. By the time that trial commenced, Christie, who was the principal witness for the prosecution, had already murdered three women, and almost certainly a child as well.

It was in September 1939 that Christie commenced as a special constable in the War Reserve Police. He served in this body for four years, earning a first aid certificate and receiving two commendations. He took the required declaration: "I do solemnly and sincerely declare and affirm that I will well and truly serve our sovereign lord the King in the office of special constable for the Metropolitan Police district without favour or affection, malice or ill will; and that I will, to the best of my power, cause the peace to be kept and preserved, and prevent all offences against the persons and properties of His Majesty's subjects, and that while I continue to hold the said office I will, to the best of my skill and knowledge, discharge all the duties thereof faithfully according to law." Not bad for a man with a criminal record and who was shortly to find fame as a serial murderer.

It was during his service with the War Reserve Police that Christie met his first victim; Ruth Fuerst. When Evans and his wife moved into 10 Rillington Place in Esher in 1948 Christie was already a double murderer. He had strangled Fuerst in August 1943 and another woman named Muriel Amelia Eady in October 1944.

Ruth Fuerst was an Australian girl, 17-years-of-age. When war broke out she decided to remain in England where she worked in a munitions factory. She rented a flat which was only a short way from Rillington Place. She was a tall attractive girl, but although prostitutes frequented the area where she worked it is uncertain whether or not she took up that activity in an 'amateur' capacity. How she came to know Christie is a mystery. What is certain is that she visited Christie at Rillington Place, and it was one of such visits which proved to be her doom. At the crucial time Ethel was away visiting relatives. According to Christie, Ruth wanted sex with him. He did so and in the course of this strangled her with a piece of rope.

Having received notice that his wife was on her way home Christie hurriedly hid Ruth's body under the floorboards in the front room. After the departure of Ethel and her brother Henry Waddington, whose arrival was not expected, Christie put the clothes of Fuerst in the wash-house. He went into the garden and began digging a grave for Fuerst near the rockery. Later that night, when it was dark he told Ethel that he was going to the lavatory and carried the body into the garden. In his subsequent statement Christie said:

> "I put the body down the hole and covered it up quickly with earth. The next day I straightened the garden and raked it over. There was an old dustbin in the garden with holes in it which I used for burning garden refuse. As I was burning rubbish I got the idea into my head to burn the clothing and what I could pull out I put it into the dust bin and burnt it. Months later I was digging in the garden and I probably misjudged where it was or something

like that. I found the skull and put it in the dust bin and covered it up. I dug a hole in the corner of the garden and put the dust bin in the hole about 18 inches down. The top of the dust bin was open and I still used it to burn the rubbish."

It is worth remembering the brutal callousness with which Christie carried out these wicked crimes in the light of his later admission regarding his murder of Beryl Evans, and his denial that he killed the baby Geraldine. Here was a man who was capable of snuffing-out the life of a defenceless human being in contrast to Evans who adored his child.

With the death of Ruth Fuerst, Christie's savage lust was far from sated. In 1944 he commenced work in the Ultra-Radio works at Park Royal in Acton. It was in the canteen that he met a girl by the name of Muriel Amelia Eady. She was 31-years-old and a spinster of perfectly good character who lived with her aunt in Putney. Her father, who was in the Merchant Navy, was away at sea. She was short with brown hair and brown eyes and on the plump side. He understood from her that she had made a friend and invited them both to 10 Rillington Place to take tea with himself and his wife.

Christie was attracted by his new discovery and with diabolical cunning he began to plan for her a similar fate as that which had befallen Ruth Fuerst. When Ethel decided to spend the holiday in Sheffield with her brother, Christie saw his opportunity. Muriel suffered from chronic catarrh and when Christie said that he possessed a useful device which could cure her condition she accepted his invitation to try it out. It was a fatal decision. Confident of his good character due to his police service she visited 10 Rillington Place where she was provided with a glass jar with a metal screw top. The jar contained Friars Balsam, but a pipe which fed gas from a tap in the room was also part of the contraption. Soon Amelia lost consciousness and Christie carried her to a bed where, as with Ruth, he had intercourse with her and at the same time strangled her to death.

This was the man who, with his wife Ethel, was to be the neighbour of Timothy Evans and his wife Beryl when they moved into 10 Rillington

Place in 1948. For a while they went to live with Evans' mother, Mrs Probert, so named because she had married again.

Mr and Mrs Probert shared the house with a married daughter and step-daughter. It was a happy arrangement and there was mutual love and affection. However, Beryl Evans was soon expecting a child and she and Timothy wanted a place of their own. They decided upon 10 Rillington Place where they took the top floor rooms. Nothing could cast a favourable light on the dreadful dreary gloom of the house which was the scene of the unspeakable events which took place there; the description given in the *Notable British Trials* series is of "a dilapidated little three-storey house known as 10 Rillington Place, North Kensington … a tiny shabby house, where the paint needed renewing, where there was no bathroom and only one water closet on the garden level for all the inhabitants."

The Evans's bought their furniture on a hire purchase contract for which Mrs Probert stood security. Beryl does not seem to have had much taste, or else no money with which to gratify it. Though her husband's family found her an alternative flat, she might have moved to a ground floor flat with a garden and water-closet of its own, she did not want to make the change. She said, "We have got everything nice up here now and the Christies are alright."

With overtime Timothy made up his earnings to seven pounds or eight pounds but he had payments on rent and hire purchase to meet and these were apt to be late. The premises are aptly described in the *Notable British Trials* series:

> "Being a cul-de-sac Rillington Place was the national playground—and still is under its new name—of the children of the neighbourhood, both black and white they tumble together on the pavements and in the street, playing with such things as empty tins, but, as children can be, they are happy enough, though in winter they must feel very cold.
>
> No 10 is the last house on the left hand side and when the Evans's had the top floor a Mr Kitchener had the middle floor and Mr and Mrs Reginald Christie had the ground floor. There are no cellars, the staircase is very narrow, and it is impossible for anybody to go much about the house without

Introduction: The Trial of Timothy Evans

the other habitants hearing. On the ground floor there is an ugly Victorian bay window to the front room of the house surrounded by crumbling sandstone. This room the Christies used as their sitting room; their bedroom was behind it with the bedroom looking out on the back yard and the garden; and a tiny kitchen, a mere box of a room, was beyond it on the other side of the narrow passage which led out to the garden and the communal water closet. This sounds as though the Christies had quite a large flat, but it must be remembered that everything was on a very small scale; the stairs very narrow; the passage between the stairs and the Christies' rooms narrower still. The Evans's top floor rooms consisted of a bedroom which was in the front and which was slightly shorter than the Christies' front room by lack of a bow window but wider because there was no passage. Their back room was their living room kitchen and the same size as Christie's bedroom. It is of importance that in front of the bay window on the ground floor there was a man-hole cover of heavy iron set into the paving over the drains which were set into the front wall beneath the window. Below the level of the sitting-room, was a ventilator grating."

It is extraordinary that a woman like Beryl, who had worked in the environment of Park Lane and while perhaps not belonging to such surroundings had become familiar with them, should be content to settle into such depressing and shabby environs. Nevertheless at first the Evans's lived together fairly amicably. There was a problem when a girl named Lucy, a friend of Beryl, came to live with them at Beryl's invitation. Since the accommodation was so limited this meant that the two women and the baby slept in the bedroom while Timothy slept on the kitchen floor. This soon became a cause of contention between Timothy and Beryl and Mrs Probert told Lucy to leave. When she did so Timothy went with her but returned after two days to his wife and child.

A far greater cause of trouble arose when Beryl found herself to be pregnant again. She told Timothy that she did not want any more children and would have an abortion. According to him, Timothy was angry about this. Beryl told her husband that she would go with the baby to Brighton to stay with her father, and on the 11th November Evans consulted a furniture dealer to collect the contents of the flat for the sum of £40. It is plain that at this point the marriage was virtually at an end.

Beryl already regarded Christie as a trustworthy man. She would have thought otherwise had she known he was already a double murderer. When Christie was told by Beryl that she wanted an abortion he saw his chance to indulge his perverted lust once again. Timothy too had fallen for Christie's lies that he was an accomplished abortionist, and since he had ceased to resist his wife's demands he was content to let matters take their course.

The details of how, when Timothy was elsewhere, Christie murdered Beryl is open to doubt. That he did so is without question since he himself had admitted as much in more than one statement. But Christie was as incapable of giving a truthful account of anything as Evans himself. The difference between them was that Christie was a homicidal maniac, Evans was not.

At his trial the statement of Christie relating to his killing of Beryl Evans was read to the court:

> "That evening Evans went out with the blonde [Lucy] and he was carrying a suitcase. He came back again later. The next day Mrs Evans told my wife that she was going down to the police court to get a separation from her husband. My wife and I had a chat and we agreed between us that if they separated we would adopt the baby, but Mrs Evans told my wife that if they did separate his mother would take the baby. At a later period Mrs Evans told me that her husband was knocking her about and that she was going to make an end of it, meaning that she was going to commit suicide.
>
> One morning shortly after this, it would be early November, I found Mrs Evans lying on a quilt in front of the fireplace in the kitchen. She had made an attempt to gas herself, and I opened the door and window wide because there was a lot of gas in the room. There was a gas pipe on the left hand side of the fireplace with a tap about two feet six inches from the floor at about the level of the top of the kitchen fireplace. There was a piece of rubber tubing from the tap to near her head. She was lying with her head towards the window. She was fully dressed and was not covered over with anything.

Introduction: The Trial of Timothy Evans

When I opened the door and window she started coming round. I gave her a drink of water. I do not know what she said, but a little while after she complained of a headache, and I made her a cup of tea. My wife was downstairs but I did not call her or tell her. Mrs Evans asked me not to tell anyone. Mr Evans was out and I don't know if there was anyone else in the house. I had a cup of tea too, because my head was thumping as I had got the effect of it [the gas] too. After a while I went downstairs.

The next day I went upstairs again, I couldn't say it was morning or afternoon, I think it was about lunch-time. She still said she intended to do away with herself. I am certain that there was a small fire in the grate in the kitchen where I found Mrs Evans the day before, and that's why I rushed to open the window.

When I went up to Mrs Evans at lunch-time the next day she begged of me to help her go through with it, meaning to help her commit suicide. She said she would do anything if I would help her. I think she was referring to letting me be intimate with her. She brought the quilt from the front room and put it down in front of the fireplace. I am not sure whether there was a fire in the grate. She lay on the quilt. She was fully dressed. I got on my knees but found I was not physically capable of having intercourse with her owing to the fact that I had fibrosis in my back and enteritis, we were both fully dressed. I turned the gas tap on and as near as I can make out, I held it close to her face. When she became unconscious I turned the tap off. I was going to try again to have intercourse with her, but it was impossible, I couldn't bend over. I think that's when I strangled her. I think it was with a stocking I found in the room. The gas wasn't on very long, not much over a minute, I think. Perhaps one or two minutes I think I left her where she was and went downstairs. She didn't know anything about it.

Evans came home in the evening about 6 o'clock. It was dark when I heard him come in. I went to my kitchen door and called him. I spoke to him in the passage and told him that his wife had committed suicide. That she had gassed herself. I went upstairs with him. We went into the kitchen, and Evans touched his wife's hand, then picked her up and carried her into the bedroom then put her on the bed. It was dark there were no lights on in the kitchen or the bedroom. I feel certain it was a stocking I strangled her with. I didn't tie it round the neck. I just wound it round the neck. Before I went downstairs I think I took the stocking off and threw it in the fireplace. I think there was a fire in the grate, I did not feel any effects of the gas.

After Evans laid his wife on the bed, he fetched the quilt from the kitchen and put it over her. I then lit the gas in the centre of the room the front room which is used as the bedroom. I told Evans that no doubt he would be suspected of having done it because of the rows and fights he had had with his wife. He seemed to think the same. He said he would bring the van down that he was driving and take her away and leave her somewhere. I left him and went downstairs. I think this was on a Tuesday and on the following Friday Evans sold his furniture, and after my wife had given him some dinner he left saying he was going to Bristol.

At that time I was under the impression that he had taken his wife away in his van. I didn't go into the bedroom that day until Evans came home in the evening. I can't recollect seeing the body there. I think Evans told me next day that he had fed the baby. Evans called at the house some days later, but only stayed a few minutes. I had my coat on ready to go to the doctor's and we left the house together and both got on a number 7 bus, I paid the fares. I got off the bus near the doctor's, and Evans stayed on the bus to go to Paddington.

Early in December the police called at the house and said they were making enquiries about Mrs Evans. There were three officers: Detective Sergeant Corfield, Detective Byers, and I think, Inspector Black. They told me that they had got Evans in Wales and that he had made a statement that he had put his wife down a drain. They said they had already had the drain up before they came to the door. They asked me to go to Notting Hill police station [to] make a statement, I went with them in a car, I stayed there from 11 pm till five in the morning. When I got back I found that they had taken a statement from my wife. They left a policeman there all night and came again the next day and made a search. They found something in

Introduction: The Trial of Timothy Evans

the outhouse and asked my wife to go to the outhouse (wash house). She told me afterwards that they pointed to a bundle and asked her if she knew anything about it.

She said she did not and they asked her to touch it to see if she knew what it was. She said she touched it but didn't know what it was and had never seen it there before. An officer told us soon after they had found a body: When I left Evans in the bedroom on that Tuesday evening he did not know that his wife had been strangled. He thought she had gassed herself. I don't know when he first found out that his wife had been strangled. I never mentioned it to him. I never had intercourse with Mrs Evans at any time. We were just friendly acquaintances, nothing more. I went up that first afternoon to have a cup of tea as she had previously asked me once or twice. I believe it was a couple of days previously that she had asked me to go up and get some sugar she had saved up for me. When I was up there she said she had just made a cup of tea and asked me to have one. I had a cup of tea with her then and she told me to come up anytime I wanted a cup of tea.

The wash-house was a communal one but usually it was only used for keeping rubbish and junk in, there was no key to it and the lock was broken and not usable. It could be opened and shut by turning the handle but could not be locked. The wash house was only used for getting water to rinse out pails to put down the lavatory.

I had some shoring timber and old floor boards which had been left by people. I asked Evans to take it to the yard for me as I could not carry it owing to my fibrositis. He took it to the yard and suggested I put it in the wash-house out of the way. I saw it in the wash-house afterwards and some of it was stacked in front of the sink. I don't think it was possible to get to the tap after the timber was put in there.

I feel certain I strangled Mrs Evans and I think it was with a stocking. I did it because she appealed to me to help her commit suicide. I have got in the back of my mind there was some other motive, but I am not clear about it. I don't know anything about what happened to the Evans' baby. I don't recall seeing the baby on the Tuesday or at anytime afterwards. It was about this time that my dog had been digging in the garden and found a skull from the body of the woman Eady that I had buried in the nearest corner of the garden. I just covered it up with earth and later in the evening when it was dark I put my raincoat on. I went into the garden and got the skull and put it under my raincoat. I went out and put it in a bombed house the last standing bombed house near the tennis courts in St Mark's Road. There was corrugated iron covering some bay windows and I dropped the skull through the window where the iron had been bent back. I heard it drop with a dull thud as though there were no floor boards.

I gassed the three women whose bodies were found in the alcove, by getting them to sit in the deck chair in the kitchen between the table and the door. There is a gas pipe on the wall next to the window that at one time had been used as a gas bracket. The pipe had been plugged, I took the plug out and pushed a piece of rubber tubing over the pipe and let it hang down nearly to the floor. There was no tap on it so I put a kink in the tube with a bulldog clip to stop the gas from escaping. When they sat in the deck chair with the tube behind them I just took the clip off and let the fumes rise from the back of the deck chair. When they started getting overcome that's when I must have strangled them.

The pubic hair found in the tin at 10 Rillington Place came from three women in the alcove and from my wife, I feel certain of this, but I can't remember when or how I took it."

This statement of Christie, one of three, was made on the 5th of June 1953 and is full of falsity. There is not a word relating to the fact that Christie had claimed to be an expert abortionist and had told Beryl that he had always been successful on previous occasions. The story that Beryl Evans had been attempting to commit suicide and that Christie was helping her to do so is no doubt another lie. It is almost certainly untrue that he did not have intercourse with her, and the injuries that she suffered to her head and face are consistent with blows he inflicted when she realised what was happening and began to struggle. The instrument

Introduction: The Trial of Timothy Evans

which he used to strangle her was most likely a piece of rope and not a stocking. In this statement, Christie says that he told Evans, when he returned that evening, that his wife had committed suicide. According to Evans what Christie said to him on his return to 10 Rillington Place was, "Its bad news. It didn't work."

Christie was completely concealing the fact that his whole plan from the beginning was to kill Beryl and in doing so to satisfy his maniacal sexual lust, as he had done with the previous killings. While it is true to say that both Evans and Christie were compulsive liars, there is an important difference between them. Christie was possessed of a demonic skill as is seen by the ingenuity with which he trapped his victims. The lies, which were associated with his murders, were smooth and plausible to a man of Evan's severely limited intelligence. Evans had a mentality of a boy of ten-and-a-half and told lies that were so absurd as to be laughable at times. He was completely under the influence of the clever and ruthless Christie. He believed Christie when he said he would dispose of the body of Beryl by putting it down a drain and no doubt also when Christie said the baby Geraldine had been taken to be looked after by a young couple in East Acton.

On the evening of November 14th, Evans, having sold his furniture, left for Wales. He arrived at Merthyr Vale the next morning and went to stay at the home of his uncle and aunt Mr and Mrs Lynch. He told them that Beryl and the baby were staying with Beryl's father at Brighton. He also told the Lynches that he and his boss were touring the West Country looking for new branches.

The stories were believed by the Lynches and Evans stayed with them for six days. Although this provided him with some relaxation, he was under considerable strain. Christie had frightened Evans by telling him that having participated in accepting Christie's offer of abortion and in helping to dispose of Beryl's body he was an accomplice to a very serious criminal offence which would land him in prison for a long time.

Evans returned to London and went to 10 Rillington Place where he spoke to Christie and asked about the baby. Christie fobbed him off by saying that he would see the baby again in two or three weeks' time.

Evans clearly thought the child was alive. Christie knew better. The baby, by that time, had been strangled like her mother.

Evans, having received no clear information regarding his baby daughter Geraldine, returned to Wales but by now it was becoming increasingly difficult to explain away the absence of Beryl. Both his sister and stepsister had visited 10 Rillington Place but failed to contact Beryl Evans and Evans once again changed his story about her to Mr and Mrs Lynch. Then came a letter from Mrs Probert to the Lynches saying that she did not believe a word her son had said. Evans had had enough. He went to the police station in Merthy Tydfil and said, "I want to give myself up. I have disposed of my wife."

The sequence of statements made by Evans was described by Christmas Humphreys, prosecuting counsel in Evans trial:

> "He thereafter made four separate statements the first of which is a long story, most of which he later said was untrue. Then he changed that first story into a second story in which he laid the whole blame with regards to the charge of the murder of the child on the shoulders of Mr Christie, who was living on the ground floor, saying he had killed his wife in the process of performing an illegal operation. Then he again changes his story and makes a verbal confession which he signs, and finally he ends up by making a long written statement saying in detail how and why he murdered his wife and child."

We shall consider "confessions" in the chapter on the trial. Never had a trial for murder at the Old Bailey taken place in such illusory circumstances. Never has a defendant, by his own self-illusion, so much contributed to his own unjust conviction; never has the main witness for the prosecution been himself a mass murderer who was in all probability guilty of the crime for which the defendant was standing trial.

CHAPTER 21

The Opening Submissions

The trial of Timothy John Evans was one of the most extraordinary ever to take place at the Old Bailey. In outward appearances it bore little difference from many other trials for murder. But the underlying fact was that the defendant stood charged with a crime of which not he, but the principal witness for the prosecution, was guilty. It was the stuff of crime fiction, yet none of the persons mainly involved in the trial, judge counsel or jury were aware of this.

The Judge's Ruling

The judge, Mr Justice Lewis, was an experienced judge of criminal cases, but he was a sick man who in fact died a short while after the case was over. Whether or not the state of his health affected his judgement is debatable. In any event he leant in favour of the prosecution. This was perhaps not surprising since Evans had made an admission, in his written statement to the police, that he had murdered his daughter Geraldine. As well as his wife.

Counsel for the prosecution was Christmas Humphreys. Travers Christmas Humphreys QC was the son of a distinguished criminal barrister and judge Sir Richard Somers Travers Christmas Humphreys. The former prosecutor had appeared in a number of important cases. In private life he was a prominent Buddhist and wrote extensively on the subject of that religion. Tall and somewhat gaunt in appearance he was an able and incisive counsel.

After the Second World War Humphreys was an assistant prosecutor at the war crimes trials in Tokyo. At the Old Bailey he was first Treasury Counsel and latterly a judge. Humphreys style of advocacy was calm and unemotional, perhaps contributed to by his Buddhism. He rarely became ruffled and never excited. He exhibited an aura of control and competence combined with a touch of dry humour.

Counsel for Evans was Mr Malcolm Morris QC. Morris was an impressive figure in court; tall and handsome he had the advantage of a strong, cultured voice and impeccable courtroom manners. Yet it would not be an injustice to say that he never ranked in the forefront of the great advocates at the English Bar. The Golden Age of the Bar, as it sometimes called, was past. Legendary names such as Edward Marshall Hall, henry Curtis-Bennett, Charles Russell, Norman Birkett and Patrick Hastings were figures of the past. They enjoyed a celebrity status which no longer applied to their successors.

It sometimes happens, during the course of a trial that an issue arises regarding the admissibility of evidence. The jury is normally asked to retire since it is not appropriate for them to attend until the judge has ruled upon it. The subject of an argument in this case could not have been more important.

Evans was charged with the murder of his baby daughter Geraldine. He had also been charged on another indictment with the murder of his wife, but the prosecution elected to proceed against him only on the charge relating to the child. Evans pleaded not guilty to the murder of the child, but Humphreys argued that, nevertheless, evidence relating to the murder of the wife, Beryl, should be admitted because it had occurred reasonably near to the same time as the killing of the child, and by the same method, namely strangulation. Therefore, it was said by counsel, the two murders were part of the same transaction.

It was plain that if such evidence was admitted it would be a devastating blow to the defence because it would be impossible to disassociate the two homicides. If they were satisfied Evans had committed the one they would almost certainly convict him of the other.

Humphreys put his argument as follows:

The Opening Submissions

"My Lord there are two indictments in this case against this man, one for murdering his wife and the other for murdering his child two days later in exactly the same circumstances by strangulation and putting the bodies in the same place. There is one set of depositions, and these depositions include the facts which concern the wife and the facts concerning the child. I have chosen to proceed upon the second and the later indictment for the murder of the child, and in my submission, all the evidence concerning the murder of the wife is admissible on the ground that is part of the same transaction.

The evidence before the court consists of a series of four statements the first of which is virtually abandoned at a later stage in favour of the second. The second alleges that the murder of the wife was really committed by a man called Christie in the course of an abortion. That is virtually entirely disregarded in favour of a verbal statement taken down by a police officer, Exhibit 8 which is a confession of the murder of the wife, and that is followed very shortly after, with a preparatory phase, I will tell you the cause of it, by a long full confession Exhibit 9, in which he related details how and why he murdered both the wife and the child.

In my submission, the evidence contained in all these statements in the depositions is admissible upon the second and later charge upon various grounds, one of which is that it is precisely the same set of facts and the same system; secondly that it is an inseparable double murder by a man who has got into a certain state of mind for the reasons given."

Malcolm Morris realised the significance for his client if this extremely damaging evidence was admitted:

"Mr Humphreys said that the evidence was that the deaths were caused on precisely the same facts and system. What he meant is a little difficult to follow, because there is no evidence that the two deaths were caused on precisely the same facts. The only evidence which there is admissible against the accused is his own last statement, and the only evidence in that statement is that on one day he says he lost his temper with his wife and strangled her, and that, having looked after his baby properly for two days subsequently, he came home two days later and strangled the baby. My Lord, I hesitate to believe that my learned friend is suggesting that an alleged confession about the murder of his wife on the 8th November is evidence of system; that is taking the law very much further than it has ever been taken before. He has described it to your Lordship as an inseparable double murder, and then, perhaps looking rather carefully to find something which is separable, he has discovered one piece in the evidence of Inspector Jennings where Inspector Jennings referred to 'their'."

Malcolm Morris then came to the hub of his objection:

"It is clear that where you have two indictments, which are severable it is prejudicial on the trial of a man with regard to the second indictment that the jury should know that at some time he has said that he strangled his wife two days before, that even if it might be argued that could be admitted as part of the transaction your Lordship, in the exercise of your discretion [you] should say in the interests of justice perhaps it is better that it should be left out; if the prosecution were proceeding on the other indictment [murder of the wife] the alleged murder of the baby would be a matter of singularly little importance, because that is something which happened subsequently, and it is quite clear that however this matter arose, and whoever is responsible for the deaths, it was the wife who dies first, and that indeed, appears to be the case for the prosecution; I ask your Lordship to say that what can be severed must be severed and that the only evidence which the prosecution are entitled to bring on this matter against the accused is the evidence which directly bears on whether or not he murdered the child, with which murder he is charged."

In his reply Christmas Humphreys said:

"My Lord, I must respectfully reiterate that in my submission, the whole of this evidence must be admissible upon this indictment, and indeed, it is going to be extremely difficult for the jury to do justice when I must talk about the wife one day as being there and the baby in the pram and the next day she is not. The jury will want to know what has happened to the wife, and why, suddenly in the middle of the story the accused man starts feeding and looking after the baby. It is going to make a limping, lame and altogether impossible story to fit together and puzzling to the jury, whereas it is one story and should so be given. He went to the police after receiving a letter from his mother, who gives the lie to the story he has been telling about the baby having gone to Brighton. That apparently affects his mind, he cannot keep it any longer, and he goes to the police and says I want to give myself up. I have disposed of my wife, and then starts telling the story about having put her down the drain, and so on. If I am to do this without this evidence, then why has he gone to the police? The jury will know that it is a patchwork of unrelated items of evidence, and very difficult to make sense of and understand."

Mr Justice Lewis decided to admit the evidence regarding Beryl Evans. He had a perfectly good reason for doing so. Yet his ruling struck the death knell for the defence. Now the jury was bound to know that there was another indictment for murder against Evans, although for reasons of their own the prosecution had decided not to proceed with it. Evans' position was little better than if both indictments for murder of his wife and child had gone ahead. If that was the case for the Crown it is hard to see why the charge of murder of Beryl Evans was discontinued. The consequences for Evans were now grim, but for justice itself they were far worse. The jury was bound to be convinced that Evans had murdered his wife, an appalling crime to which Christie, the Crown's principal witness would one day plead guilty. Since he was ultimately held to be guilty of the murder of the child the ultimate result was the execution of an innocent man.

The task now facing defending counsel was hopelessly uphill. Evans had made several conflicting statements, one of which had been a confession to the murders of Beryl and Geraldine. The defence was that Christie was, when presented in court, innocent, a man whose only previous offences had been committed a long while ago and were minor compared with the allegations being made against him. He was put before the jury as having served his country in the First World War when he had received a serious wound. He had also been a member of the police in the Second World War and received commendations. Not only did Malcolm Morris have to provide a convincing explanation as to why Evans had admitted to the shocking crimes which he had not committed, but he was obliged to attempt to substantiate the accusations made by his client that an apparently respectable, law-abiding citizen who had attended court to give evidence was the guilty party.

The problem for an advocate is clear. If he puts the allegations too apologetically it will appear that he has little confidence in his client's veracity. If, on the other hand, he attacks the prosecution witness aggressively he will seem to be bullying. Mr Morris did his best with a well-nigh impossible brief, but there could be little doubt regarding the outcome.

CHAPTER 22

The Prosecution Case

Having won the ruling on the evidence, prosecuting counsel made full use of his advantage:

"May it please you my Lord. Members of the jury, the accused is charged with the murder of his small daughter aged 14 months. They lived at an address in Rillington Place, Notting Hill Gate, London. On the ground floor were a Mr and Mrs Christie, who will be called as witnesses in this case; on the first floor there was, when he was there, a Mr Kitchener, who was at this time in hospital, and on the second floor lived the accused man, his wife and baby. The case for the Crown is that this man and his wife got on badly, that he got depressed because he lost his job and that he got more and more depressed, and that then as he himself said, he killed his wife then killed the child. In order to account for the fact that he had killed them, he lied to various neighbours and relations as to where they were, because he had to account for their sudden absence from home.

He then went to Wales, and in Wales he was shown by an aunt a letter from his mother exposing the lies he had been telling about the whereabouts of the child, and as a result he went to the police and began making statements to them. He thereafter made four separate statements, the first of which is a long story, most of which he later said was untrue. Then he changed that first story into a second story in which he laid the whole blame with regard to the murder of the child on the shoulders of Mr Christie, who was living on the ground floor, saying he had killed his wife in the process of performing an illegal operation. Then he again changed his story and made a verbal confession which he signs, and finally he ends up by making a long written statement saying in detail why and how he murdered his wife and the child.

That is the outline of the case for the prosecution, and it is for you when you have heard the evidence, to decide whether in fact this man murdered his baby."

Humphreys then outlined the evidence which he proposed to call. It presented a grim picture for Evans:

"Very roughly the sequence of events that you are gong to hear [about] from the witness is as follows. On the 8th November at lunchtime the wife and baby are seen by Mr Christie, they are never seen alive again. That night Mr and Mrs Christie hear a bump or a thud in the flat above their heads. The next morning the accused alone is seen by Mrs Christie and she asked about the wife and baby. He said vaguely that he is by himself and that they may have gone to Bristol. He begins to tell lies about them. On the next day, 10th November, both the Christies again see him. They see he is looking rather wild, he says he has packed up his job, and he talks about having a row with his governor. On the 11th November he is telling Mr Christie he is going to sell his furniture and three days later sure enough a van arrives, and he sells the furniture for £40. He then goes down to his aunt in Wales and tells her that his wife has gone to Brighton.

He then comes up to London again and sees Mr Christie, and tells him that he could not get a job. Christie gives him some advice and a day or two later he goes back to Wales and sees his aunt and tells her more lies to the effect that he had seen his wife and she had walked out of the flat, and so on, and that he had given the baby to some friends at Newport to look after.

Then comes the letter, because the aunt had written to the mother in London who was in close touch with her son, about what he was saying he had done. The answer comes back from the mother, and it is read out to the accused man. That gave the lie to some of the stories he was telling, and it would seem that it was [as] a result of that letter being read out that he changed his mind and went straight to the police in Merthyr Tydfil and said 'I want to give myself up. I have disposed of my wife.' He told them all about it, and how he had pushed her down the drain. They say it is not very likely and he says I know what I am saying. I want to get it off my chest. I cannot sleep and so on, and he then makes a statement Exhibit 6. I will not read it to you in detail, but it says that his wife was expecting a baby (which was in fact true), that he met a man who was driving a lorry in a café somewhere, that the man had some wonderful stuff to bring about an abortion of a woman who did not want to have a baby, and gave him a bottle, that he gave to his wife something out of the bottle, and to his horror he found that she was dead. He said that he put her down a drain, and so on, told various lies to account for his actions, and then went to the country. Which I suggest is the only part of the statement which is true.

The police telephoned London to have enquiries made and to have this drain searched, and one came back to him and said 'Well the drain you say you put your wife's body in has been examined and there is nothing there' he replied 'Well, I put it there'. The police officer said 'So it is a man hole?' and he replied 'I expect so' the officer said 'Who helped you lift the lid off?' And he replied 'I did it myself.' The officer said 'I don't think you are physically capable of taking the lid off a man-hole, it was as much as three men can do.' And he replied 'Well I did it myself'". The officer said 'I don't think your wife's body has ever been in the drain' and he said 'No. I said that to protect a man named Christie. It is not true about the man in the café either, I'll tell you the truth now' and he proceeded to make another statement, Exhibit 7."

This in brief is an attack upon the fellow lodger Christie, saying virtually that it was Christie who had given some tablets to his wife, that his wife had taken one of these and died, that it was Christie who had taken upon himself the burden of removing the body of the woman for whose death he was responsible, saying that he would put the body in the empty flat of Mr Kitchener, "which you remember was on the first floor of the same house, and that he afterwards made arrangements for the baby to be looked after by a young couple in Acton. He now says the baby is at East Acton, whereas it is in fact still in the house."

Evans' story was that he came home that night and was told by Christie that the people had called for the baby, and that he, Christie, had put the body of his wife down the drain. He finished by saying that he saw his mother and repeated these lies to her, that they had gone to Brighton and that then Christie had told him that the best thing to do was to sell the furniture and clear out. Then he said he met a rag-and-bone man and told him there were a lot of things in his place that he could have, and he proceeded to tear up his wife's clothing and other things and gave them to the rag-and-bone man.

> "The police, having heard the second story on the 1st December they go back to him and ask him more, they say 'When did you last see your wife's body?' And he replies 'just before Christie took it to Kitchener's flat', they press him and ask him 'did you help Christie to carry it down?' And he says that finding Christie having heavy weather getting the dead body downstairs, he helped him and he says 'that's the truth. That's the last time I saw the body'. He is asked 'When did you arrive at Merthyr Vale?' And he says 'Tuesday the 14th'. The police then say 'Have you been back there since?' And he says 'Oh yes. I forgot about that. I went back on Wednesday or Thursday after I came down. I walked back to see about my child. I called at Christie's and asked where my child was and he said "She is alright. You can't see her yet, it would be too early. Leave her alone for about two or three weeks. Then write to me and I'll let you know when you can see her". That is all in support of the second story that he told, that Christie had arranged that the body should be taken to Kitchener's flat."

Humphreys continued:

> "We now come to the 2nd December, when, as a result of these conflicting statements and further enquiries by the police, the police go to this house and search. In an outhouse on the ground floor at the rear they find a large package which turns out to be the strangled dead body of his wife and, what is more immediately pertinent here another small parcel which is the

strangled body of the baby, strangled with one of his own ties. The remains were examined by Dr Teare who will tell you that the woman had been strangled, that she was in fact four months pregnant and that he could find no evidence of interference with the pregnancy; and the baby in the same way had been strangled by a tie tied tightly round her neck—not a difficult thing to do with a baby of fourteen months.

The accused man was brought to London that night, and Chief Inspector Jennings said to him 'I found the dead body of your wife concealed in a wash-house at 10 Rillington Place, Notting Hill, also the body of your baby daughter Geraldine, in the same outbuilding. And this clothing was found on them. Later today I was present at Kensington Mortuary, when it was established that the cause of death was strangulation in both cases. I have reason to believe that you were responsible for causing their deaths', the accused man said 'Yes' and he was therefore immediately cautioned by the police officer and told he need not say anything if he did not wish to, but anything he did say would be taken down in writing and might be given in evidence."

Chief Inspector Jennings then said that Evans made a statement which the officer wrote down following which Evans signed it, so that it had the value of a statement made by him:

"She was incurring one debt after another and I could not stand it any longer so I strangled her with a piece of rope and took her down to the flat below the same night while the other man was in hospital. I waited till the Christies downstairs had gone to bed, then took her to the wash-house after midnight. This was on Tuesday 8th November. On Thursday evening after I came home from work I strangled my baby in our bedroom with my tie, and later that night I took her down into the wash-house after the Christie's had gone to bed."

"You will notice," said Jennings, "that he is completely abandoning the allegation that Christie was the murderer and completely abandoning the allegation that Christie had anything to do with the abortion, frankly saying that he was the murderer of these two persons, and where he had put their bodies, and though he did not know it then, the tie which he said he used and was found round the baby's neck."

"He signed that, and in case it is thought by anybody that this was signed excitedly or out of bravado, he said it is great relief to get it off my chest. I feel better already, and he went further and said 'I can tell you the cause that led up to it'. He was again cautioned and told that he need not say anything and asked if he wished what he said to be written down, and he said 'Yes'. It was written down and signed and appears [as] Exhibit 9. The first part is a long and detailed account of the rows he was always having with his wife, and then he says 'I got home about 10.30 pm. I walked in and she started to row again so I went straight to bed. I got up Tuesday morning and went straight to work. I came home at night about 6.30 pm, my wife started to argue again, so I hit her across the face with the [flat of my] hand. She then hit me back with her hand. In a fit of temper I grabbed a piece of rope from the chair which I had brought home off my van and strangled her with it. I then took her into the bedroom and laid her on the bed with the rope still tied round her neck. Before 10 pm that night I carried my wife's body downstairs to the kitchen of Mr Kitchener's flat as I knew he was away in hospital'. Then he describes how he looked after the baby that night, and the next two days feeding it and keeping it clean and looking after it quite well, but after two days he had an argument with his governor and he left the job and that apparently upset him very much 'I told him I wanted to post some money off to my wife first thing in the morning. He asked me where my wife was, I told him she had gone to Bristol on a holiday. He said 'How do you intend to send the money to her? I said 'In a registered envelope'. 'He paid me the money £20 he said "you can call over tomorrow for your cards"'— and he was then dismissed, 'I then went home picked up my baby from her cot in the bedroom, picked up my tie and strangled her with it. I then put the baby back in the cot and sat down in the kitchen and waited for the Christies downstairs to go to bed. At about 12 o'clock that night I took the baby downstairs to the wash-house and hid her body behind some wood. I then locked the wash-house behind me and came in closing the back door behind me. I then slipped back upstairs and laid on the bed all night fully clothed'; then he described for the third time how he sold his furniture and went down to Merthyr Tydfil and stayed with his aunt.

There is little more to tell. On the 3rd December in the morning he was seen in London by Chief Inspector Jennings, 'You are going to be charged with the murder of Beryl Susanna Evans—that was his wife by strangulation and he said 'Yes. That's right'. Later when he was charged with that offence and also in relation to the baby, he was again cautioned that he need not say anything and he made no reply."

Humphreys then concluded as follows:

"Members of the jury, there are two matters in the case, the killing of the wife with which you are not concerned, and the killing of the baby. His Lordship has ruled that the whole of these facts are part and parcel of the same circumstances surrounding the death of the baby. You are concerned with the death of the baby. It is alleged that he murdered the baby deliberately, as he himself set out not once but twice. For you will have to consider whether you have any doubt that the story that he there told was true. You will bear in mind that he begins with a story most of which he abandons, and that he goes on to tell another story, which is a terrible accusation, if it is true, of the murder by a man downstairs of his wife, and he then throws both these statements away and clearly confesses to the murder of his wife and child. You will listen to the evidence of the witness for the prosecution and you will listen to any defence which the accused may put forward, through his counsel or by any other witness he may call, but when you have heard the whole of the evidence you may well think—and indeed you must be certain in your minds that it is so—that he murdered his baby, and in that case you will find him guilty of wilful murder, as set out with this indictment."

It might be well to pause at this point and take an overview of the evidence against Evans. This is firstly the testimony of Christie, which was incriminating of Evans but a denial of Evans' accusation involving himself? And secondly of Evans four statements: the first was to the police in Wales the second two to the London police. These successively constituted an admission first that his wife had died from a dose of a potion given him by a stranger in order to abort her baby and that Christie had attempted to abort her and killed her as a result. The second two statements were a confession of murder of both his wife and child.

After formal evidence relating to the layout of 10 Rillington Place Mr Humphreys called Dr Robert Teare who gave his evidence that Beryl and Geraldine both died by strangulation, in the case of Geraldine by a tie, in the case of Beryl with a piece of rope. Beryl Evans was approximately 16 weeks pregnant at the time of her death.

Then the prosecution called John Reginald Halliday Christie. As noted earlier, it has to be unique in the history of British murder trials that the main witness for the prosecution, presented as a commendable citizen, apart from a few comparatively minor offences many years ago, was in fact the serial killer of (at least) four people, two of which were the very persons whom the defendant was alleged to have strangled. Christie described the flats and their occupants and the accessibility of the back yard and the wash-house from Evans' flat on the upstairs floor. Needless to say, Christie lied throughout regarding his own part in the events leading up to the two deaths. Christie was examined in chief by Christmas Humphreys, counsel for the Crown:

> **Christmas Humphreys:** But if any of the tenants upstairs came down in the night and wanted to get to the wash-house in the back yard they would have to pass your door?
> **John Reginald Halliday Christie:** Yes.
> **Humphreys:** And if they did not want you to know they would wait for you to go to sleep?
> **Christie:** Yes, very likely, or else when we were out.
> **Humphreys:** How may lavatories are there in the house?
> **Christie:** One. One in the back yard.
> **Humphreys:** That is the one shown beyond the wash-house?
> **Christie:** Yes.

Humphreys: Therefore if anybody living in the house wants to go to the lavatory they must come down that way?

Christie: Yes sir.

Humphreys: And therefore, that back-door as you say, is kept open or unlocked?

Christie: Yes.

Humphreys: Now, on the 8th November last year do you remember seeing Mrs Evans and the baby is that right?

Christie: On the 8th, on the Tuesday, yes.

Humphreys: Did you ever see them again?

Morris: I am sure Mr Humphreys will be most careful not to lead as to any dates in this matter.

Humphreys: I am so sorry. Did you see Mrs Evans and the baby?

Christie: Yes.

Humphreys: After that date did you ever see them again?

Christie: No sir.

Humphreys: Now coming to the next incident, at some time did you hear something in the night?

Christie: That was at midnight on the 8th, or around about midnight.

Humphreys: Wednesday–Thursday?

Christie: No. Tuesday–Wednesday.

Humphreys: The Tuesday–Wednesday midnight?

Christie: Yes.

Humphreys: What did you hear?

Christie: Well, we were both in bed, my wife and I, and we were startled in the middle of the night by a very loud thud.

Humphreys: A thud, did you say?

Christie: Yes.

Humphreys: Then what did you hear?

Christie: We listened for a few seconds and didn't hear anything, and I gradually knelt up in bed and looked through the window which overlooks the yard. It was very dark and I couldn't see anything there, and so I went back and we had laid down, and shortly after that I heard some movement which appeared to be upstairs.

Humphreys: What sort of movement?

> **Christie:** As though something was being moved, something heavy was being moved.

It was then that Mr Justice Lewis made one of a great many interruptions—some of them seemingly unnecessary: "Upstairs?" Answer "Yes it appeared to come from upstairs, I listened to that for a very short time, I suppose, and I went off to sleep, and I don't remember anything else after that."

Contrast this testimony of Christie with his own statement in June 1953:

> "When I went up to Mrs Evans at lunch-time the next day she begged me to go help her go through with it, meaning to help her commit suicide. She said she would do anything if I would help her. I think she was referring to letting me be intimate with her. She brought the quilt from the front room and put it down in front of the fireplace I am not sure whether there was a fire in the grate. She lay on the quilt, she was fully dressed. I got on my knees but found I was not physically capable of having intercourse with her owing to the fact that I have had fibrositis in my back and enteritis. We were both fully dressed. I turned the gas tap on and as near as I can make out I held it close to her face. When she became unconscious I turned the tap off. I was going again to try and have intercourse with her but it was impossible, I couldn't bend over. I think that's when I strangled her. I think it was with a stocking I found in the room. The gas wasn't on very long, not much over a minute I think. Perhaps one or two minutes. I then left her where she was and went downstairs. I think my wife was downstairs, she didn't know anything about it."

Christie's evidence was a string of lies and concealment. In answer to the judge he said that he saw Evans at 10.30 pm on the 10th November:

> **Christie:** My wife was always in the habit, if they went out at any time, to put on the hall light for them on their return, and on this particular night she went to the bedroom and said, "Wait a minute and I'll put the

light on for you" and he said "It doesn't matter I can manage" and she said "Where is Beryl and the baby?"

Mr Justice Lewis: This is your wife speaking to Evans?

Christie: Yes. I was standing in the doorway of the bedroom.

Mr Justice Lewis: You heard this conversation?

Christie: Yes my lord.

Humphreys: "Where is Beryl and the baby" what was the answer?

Christie: He said "Oh, she has gone away to Bristol".

Humphreys: Gone away to Bristol?

Christie: Yes. Away and my wife said "She never told me she was going" and he said she said she would write.

Humphreys: That was all that happened that night?

Christie: Yes and he said goodnight and went upstairs.

After more questions by the judge the examination continued:

Humphreys: When did you next see him?

Christie: On the Thursday.

Humphreys: Thursday the 10th?

Christie: I heard somebody come in, I think about half-past-six I presume it was Mr Evans, and he went straight upstairs and about a quarter of an hour afterwards he came down and knocked at my kitchen door. And I opened the door. And he stood just in the doorway; he did not come into the kitchen.

Humphreys: What did he say?

Christie: He said "I have packed in my job." He said "I have been down to Brighton and I have brought three customers' orders back, and they played hell with me."

Humphreys: What did you gather from that? I don't think it very much matters, but you do mean he ought to have brought back very much more?

Christie: He ought to have delivered all of them. He should not have brought any of them back.

Humphreys: What was he going to do, Evans?

Christie: I asked him. I said "What are you going to do now? And he said 'Well, I have got prospects of a job in Bristol and I may be going down at the weekend, and if the job come off, then I shall settle down there'."

Humphreys: How well did he seem in his manner then?

Christie: Well he seemed extremely angry, upset, really wild, as though he had a terrific row, I should imagine; he looked that way.

Humphreys: Did you see him there the next day, the Friday?

Christie: Well he was about on Friday.

Humphreys: Did he tell you anything he was going to do?

Christie: He did say he was going to—No I saw him late Friday, late Friday night.

Humphreys: Well, sometime on Friday what did he tell you he was going to do?

Christie: When he came in my wife went to put the hall light on for him again as usual, and he said it didn't matter, he could manage. The hall floor had been pulled up and there was only planking laid down and it was rotten dangerous, and he said he could manage and come along the hall, and my wife said "Have you heard from Beryl?" and he said "She has phoned me, she is alright. She is going to write to you" and he said goodnight and she said goodnight.

Humphreys: Anything about the furniture?

Christie: He mentioned that he proposed to sell his furniture get rid of his furniture, because he could not take it down to Bristol.

Humphreys: Did he say when?

Christie: At the weekend; he said he was going to see somebody.

Humphreys: Did the furniture go?

Christie: Yes. The furniture went on Monday, the 14th Mr Evans on the Sunday morning told me that he was expecting a van to come down from the furniture people to view the furniture and make an offer. On Sunday he said he expected a man to make an offer, the furniture went on Monday, and shortly after the furniture went, I should say about a quarter-of-an-hour, Mr Evans came down to the hall and called and said he was carrying a rather large suitcase, and he said he was going down to Bristol then, and he also told me that he had received £60 for the furniture, and he held out his hand and showed a roll of notes in his hand.

Humphreys: Now do you remember when you next saw him after Sunday, the 13th?

Christie: On Monday the 14th was when he went.

Humphreys: That is when the furniture goes? After that when did you next see him?

Christie: On the 23rd the Wednesday, nine days afterwards. I was just getting ready to go to my doctor's at about twenty-past or half-past-five, I think and my bell rang the front door bell. I answered the door, and Mr Evans was stood in the doorway. He said "I have just come straight down from Wales, I have come from Paddington station. I have not really seen anybody; I've come straight down here." I asked him in and said "What on earth are you doing here?" he said "Beryl has walked out on me, and I couldn't find a job, so I have been to Bristol, Cardiff, Birmingham, and Coventry and back to Cardiff and I could not find a job. I said "Well, what you should have done was settle down somewhere, paid for rooms accommodation, for a brief period of time and the money you had, that £60 would have kept you going till you got a job". He said "Well, I have had to spend a lot on travel" I said "How much have you got left" he said "About a couple of pounds". And so I told him what I thought he had done with the money. He seemed anxious to get away, and he said he was going straight back to Wales, and as he was going in the same direction as my doctor we went out together. We get on a number 7 bus in Cambridge Gardens and I got off at Portobello Road to see my doctor, and he proceeded on the bus to Paddington and I did not see him again.

Humphreys: You were under medical treatment at the time?

Christie: Yes and still am.

Humphreys: Still are; and you are not too well? What were you doing [in] the war Mr Christie?

Christie: I was a police officer during the war.

Humphreys: For how long?

Christie: From the 1st September 1939 to September 1943.

Humphreys: So for four years you were in the police.

Christie: Yes.

Humphreys: You are rather a sick man now?

Christie: Yes.

Mr Justice Lewis: You said something about your voice and gas?

Christie: Yes, that was the first war; I was in the 1914 war.

Mr Malcolm Morris rose to cross-examine Christie. Seldom, if ever could an advocate have had a worse case to contend with than that which confronted Malcolm Morris QC at the trial of Timothy Evans. It was no reflection on the ability of Morris to say that he made little progress in his attempt to expose Christie for the liar that he was or to effect a breakthrough in his performance as a witness. It must be born in mind that defending counsel laboured under several grave disadvantages.

Firstly he was representing a man who was a proven and persistent liar. He had the task of trying to persuade the jury to accept as truth the word of such a person. Secondly, his client had made two statements to the police in which he had admitted, in detail, the offence with which he had been charged, together with another allegation of murder which, although not in this particular indictment, was very much before the jury. Thirdly, Evans had changed his story several times—which one was the jury supposed to believe? Finally, and most devastating of all, the allegation which counsel was obliged to make, on the basis of his instructions, was that the very crime for which his client was called upon to answer was in fact committed by the principal prosecution witness. Finally, Christie, who unknown to the court was a multiple murderer was presented as a commendable citizen who had served his country in two wars as a soldier and as a policeman respectively.

It is a golden rule of the Bar that counsel must act upon instructions. The instruction which Malcolm Morris had received from Evans were that Christie had posed as an expert abortionist, that Beryl had died under Christies "treatment" and that he and Christie together had arranged the disposal of the body. Evans had no knowledge that Christie had murdered Beryl in a fit a sexual mania and nor, likewise, did his counsel. Everything which Malcolm Morris put to Christie met with

The Prosecution Case

denial. Did Christie know a couple in Acton? He did not. Did he tell Evans that he did? He did not.

Counsel questioned Christie at length about the tie which was found entwined around Geraldine's neck. But made no progress. Indeed, the questions put to Christie concerning the tie became so confusing and ineffective that the judge felt obliged to intervene in a manner which was far from helpful:

Malcolm Morris: Would you look at Exhibit 3? Is that your tie?
Christie: No.
Morris: Have you ever seen it before?
Christie: I saw it in the police station.
Morris: In what circumstances?
Christie: When I was taken up there with my wife to identify clothing.
Morris: To identify clothing.
Christie: Yes.
Morris: What do you mean by that?
Christie: I was taken up by the police to Notting Hill Police Station to see if I could identify clothing which was on the floor of the station belonging to Mrs Evans and the baby. I identified most of it.
Morris: Do you remember when that was?
Christie: It was in December, but I cannot recollect.
Morris: Do you remember at what time of the day?
Christie: In the evening.
Morris: About what sort of time?
Christie: I don't recollect the time.
Morris: Well. Not late at night?
Christie: No. It was not late. It was possibly about 8 o'clock I should think so far as I remember.
Morris: What was your reaction when you saw that tie?
Christie: I was asked — it was brought out of an envelope.
Mr Justice Lewis: I do not understand that.
Morris: I was asking him how he reacted.
Mr Justice Lewis: I do not understand what you mean by how he reacted:
Morris: Whether he recognised it, my Lord.

Christie: I just told you I did not recognise it. You asked me if it was my tie.

Morris: Are you saying you do not know whose tie it is?

Christie: I am not certain at all; but it is not mine.

Morris: When you say you are not certain at all do you have any idea?

Christie: Well there are only two other men in the house, that was Mr Kitchener and Mr Evans.

Mr Justice Lewis: Mr who?

Christie: Mr Kitchener; he was an elderly gentleman who was taken to hospital.

Mr Justice Lewis: He was not in the house then?

Christie: No, my Lord.

Mr Justice Lewis: He lived on the first floor and was away then?

Christie: Yes.

Morris: As I understand it, you were shown this tie at the police station?

Christie: Yes

Morris: You were not in the house, Rillington Place, at the time; you were in the police station?

Christie: Yes.

Mr Justice Lewis: He has not said so, Mr Morris?

Morris: Yes. With great respect my Lord.

Christie: I have said the first time I saw the tie I was in the police station when I was asked to identify some stuff.

Mr Justice Lewis: And he then added there were only two other men in the house, the prisoner and Mr Kitchener; but Mr Kitchener was not there at the time, he was in hospital. This meant two men were usually in the house.

Morris: But at this time he was not in the house. You were shown this tie in the police station; is that right?

Christie: Yes.

Morris: You were asked if you recognised the tie or something like that?

Christie: Yes.

Morris: And when I asked what your reaction was—I apologise if my question was not clear—what I meant was did you recognise it? I understand you said no?

Christie: No. I did not recognise it.

Morris: But in view of something that was going on in your mind about there only being two men in the house did you say anything about that tie to connect it with Evans to the police?

Christie: I think I did say I had seen Mr Evans wearing a striped tie but I could not say whether this was the one or not.

Morris: You meant by that did not you, if you meant anything, that you associated Evans at best vaguely with the tie?

Christie: Well, there was no other thing to do, whereas unless it was one of Mr Kitchener's and he was not in at the time.

Morris: But Mr Christie, you were working on the assumption that the tie which you were shown in the police station was belonging either to Evans or Kitchener or you?

Christie: It must have done.

Morris: That was the assumption on which you were working, was it?

Christie: Up to a point yes.

Morris: And you said to the police that it did not belong to you?

Christie: Yes.

Morris: That it could not belong to Kitchener or roughly that; that is what your mind said, at any rate?

Christie: Yes.

Morris: Although you had seen Evans wearing a striped tie?

Christie: Yes. I had seen him wearing a striped tie.

Morris: You are wearing a striped tie now, are you not?

Christie: Yes.

Morris: What is the point in telling the police that you had seen Evans wearing a striped tie if you could not say whether it was that tie or not?

Christie: I was asked at the time if I noticed what type of tie Mr Evans used and I said at the time that I knew I had recognised him wearing a red one very frequently, but I had seen him wearing a striped one, but what the striped one was I could not recollect.

Morris: I see. Just hold that tie up for a moment will you, you say you had seen Evans wearing a striped tie?

Christie: Yes.

Morris: This is not very obviously striped is it?

Christie: Not a great deal no.

These passages are a classic example of cross-examination which gains nothing. In fairness to Malcolm Morris it may be said that he was placed in an intensely difficult situation. He had no instructions to the effect that Christie had already murdered several persons. If he attacked the witness too aggressively there would be a danger that he might create sympathy for a man who the jury might well regards as a commendable citizen. On the other hand, if, as appears to be the case, he handled the witness too politely, the impression would be created that counsel's questioning lacked genuine purpose. But the fact remains that weak cross-examination which leaves the person subjected to it undamaged supports rather than derogates from his or her evidence. At no time did Malcolm Morris shake Christie who responded to his interrogation with skill and persistence.

Morris put the general case against Christie with something approaching courtesy:

> **Malcolm Morris:** Well, Mr Christie, I have to suggest to you, and I do not want there to be any misapprehension about it that you are responsible for the death of Mrs Evans and the little girl, or is that not so? At least that you know very much more about these deaths than you have said?
>
> **Christie:** That is a lie.

Christie denied any part played by him in the attempted abortion or death of Beryl Evans:

> **Christie:** I mentioned to Mr Evans in the presence of my wife that we understand that from what Mrs Evans told my wife that she had been taking pills and various things to procure an abortion and I discussed with my wife that we ought to advise her to stop doing that sort of thing as she was looking really ill. On that occasion we spoke to her down in my kitchen and told her that she was looking really bad and eventually she might go on and poison herself, or have some bad effect. Then she said she realised the situation and said that she would take our advice and stop taking these things.

The Prosecution Case

Christie was prepared to make concessions where this suited him:

Morris: Would that be, perhaps a week before the 8th November; round about the beginning of November or the end of October?
Christie: I should think in October.
Morris: But late in October?
Christie: Yes.
Morris: Perhaps between a week and a fortnight before?
Christie: Very likely.
Morris: Now, I suggest that at about that time or a little later, you said to Evans that you would like to have a chat with him about his wife taking those tablets. Do you remember that?
Christie: No I did not say that, but I did have a chat with him.
Morris: And was that chat about his wife taking those tablets?
Christie: Yes.
Morris: Did you say to Evans something to this effect: "You know what she is taking them for, she is trying to get rid of the baby?"
Christie: Yes.
Morris: Did you go on to say this? — "If you or your wife had come to me in the first place I could have done it for you without any risk?"
Christie: No, no, definitely not.

Christie went on to deny emphatically that he had ever offered to abort Beryl or that he had told her he had received medical training at any time. He said he had not shown a medical book to Evans to substantiate his claim to medical knowledge. Defending counsel prefaced his next questions with the somewhat apologetic statement: "Now Mr Christie, it is clear that you are going to deny what I am going to put to you now, but I must put it to you in a little detail." There followed a good deal of cross-examination regarding the builder's work at No 10 Rillington Place. Christie was questioned by Morris regarding the thud and apparent movement of furniture from the flat above. He emphatically denied taking any part in the disposal of the body of Beryl Evans or that he had ever agreed to feed baby Geraldine, which he would not know how to do anyway. Christie further denied having told Evans to say his wife and child had gone to Brighton should anyone enquire about them, nor did he advise Evans to leave London. Counsel for Evans then put to Christie his previous convictions. These had occurred 17 years before and, apart from one, were four offences of dishonesty. Finally, he denied having carried out abortions for young women or having told Evans that he had done so.

Christmas Humphreys re-examination was brief:

Christmas Humphreys: Do you appreciate that the medical evidence in this case which has been called is that this woman was strangled?

Christie: Yes. I was informed of that.

Humphreys: Not killed by abortion, but by strangulation?

Christie: Yes. I was informed of that.

Humphreys: Do you appreciate that it is being alleged that you murdered this woman?

Christie: Yes.

Humphreys: Or that you strangled her?

Christie: Yes, I was informed of that.

Humphreys: And that you strangled the baby?

Christie: Yes, I was told that.

Humphreys: Assuming that she died on the 8th November, the Tuesday night, you have told the jury what was your physical condition?

Christie: Yes.

Humphreys: That in order to pick up a pin from the floor you had to go down on all fours?

Christie: Yes. I had to.

Humphreys: Now, only a word about your character, what were you doing in the First World War?

Christie: I was in the army in the First World War.

Humphreys: Fighting for your country?

Christie: Yes. I was in the Duke of Wellington's regiment and the Notts and Derby, and I was gassed twice, and I was blinded for three months, and never spoke for three-and-a-half years.

Mr Justice Lewis: Blinded? As a result of the gas?

Christie: Yes. Mustard gas.

Mr Justice Lewis: You say you did not speak for three years?

Christie: Three-and-a-half years.

Mr Justice Lewis: The gas affected your throat?

Christie: Yes. That is why my voice is quiet at times now my Lord.

Christmas Humphreys' concluding questions were:

Humphreys: The last time you were in trouble with the police for any offence was in 1933 was it, 17 years ago?.

Christie: Yes.

Humphreys: In the last war, in spite of your disabilities, you served in the War Reserve Police for many years is that right?

Christie: Yes I did, and I was commended on two occasions.

Humphreys: And over this period in November you were suffering from your various illnesses.

Christie: Yes.

One can imagine the reactions of everyone in court if Christie had added: "I should also say that I have murdered two women whose bodies are buried in the garden of the house where I live and I shall in due course be confessing to the strangulation of Beryl Evans." The famous Bateman cartoon "The Culprit Who Admitted Everything" could not compare with it. Mrs Ethel Christie gave evidence to the effect that she heard the bump in the night and another noise of which her husband had spoken. She also said that when he asked Evans about his wife and baby he said they had gone to Bristol. Mrs Violet Gwendoline Lynch gave evidence regarding Evans' reaction to the letter from his mother.

There then followed the various statements made by Evans to the police. It was on the contents of these statements that the case against him was based and it was on the strength of these that Evans was convicted of the murder of his daughter Geraldine and was executed. It is therefore necessary to consider these accounts very carefully in order to assess what pressures this man of a retarded mentality was under when he made them, and how he brought about his own death thereby.

Detective Constable Howell Evans, stationed at Merthyr Tydfil described how Evans entered the police office on the 30th November and said, "I want to give myself up", "I have disposed of my wife." When asked, "What do you mean?" he replied, "I put her down the drain."

When the officer said, "You realise what you are saying? Just think before you say any more" Evans replied, "Yes, I know what I am saying, I can't sleep, and want to get it off my chest." Evans was then cautioned and said, "I will tell you all about it and you can write it down. I am not very educated, and cannot read or write." Evans then made his first statement to the police:

"About the beginning of October, my wife Beryl Susan Evans, told me that she was expecting a baby. She told me that she was about three months gone. I said if you are having a baby, well you've had one, another won't make any difference. She then told me she was going to try and get rid of it. I turned round and told her not to be silly, that she'd make herself ill. Then she bought herself a syringe and started syringing herself. Then she said that didn't work and I said 'I am glad it didn't work'. Then she said she was going to buy some tablets. I don't know what tablets she bought because she was always hiding them from me. She started to look very ill, and I told her to go and see a doctor, and she said she would go when I was in work; but when I came home and asked her if she had been she would always say that she hadn't. On the (Monday) Sunday morning that would be the (seventh) sixth day of November. (Alterations by Evans — final is the sixth) she told me that if she couldn't get rid of the baby she'd kill herself and our baby, Geraldine. I told her she was talking silly. She never said no more about it then, but when I got up to go to work she said she was going to see some woman to see if she could help her. Who the woman was she didn't tell me, and that if I wasn't in when she came home she'd be up at her grandmother's. Then I went to work, I loaded up my van and went on my journey. About nine o'clock that morning I pulled up at a transport café between Ipswich and Colchester. I can't say exactly where it is, I went up to the counter and ordered a cup of tea and breakfast, and I sat down by the table with my cup of tea waiting for my breakfast to come up, and there was a man sitting at the table opposite to me. He asked me if I had a cigarette I

The Prosecution Case

could give him. I gave him one and he started talking about married life. He said to me you are looking pretty worried. Is there anything on your mind?

Then I told him all about it, so he said 'Don't let that worry you, I can give you something that can fix it?' So he said 'Wait there a moment I'll be right back, and he went outside. When he came back he handed me a little bottle that was wrapped up in brown paper. He said tell your wife to take it first thing in the morning before she has any tea then to lay down on the bed for a couple of hours and that should do the job.' He never asked me for money for it. I went up to the counter and paid my bill and carried on with my journey.

After I finished my work I went home, that would be between seven and eight. When I got in the house I took off my overcoat and hung it on a peg behind the kitchen door. My wife asked me for a cigarette and I told her there was one in my packet. Then she found this bottle in my pocket and I told her all about it. Then I had my tea and sat down and read the papers and listened to the wireless. We went to bed at ten o'clock.

I got up in the morning as usual at six o'clock to go to work. I made myself a cup of tea and made a feed for the baby. I told her then not to take that stuff and I went in and said 'Good morning' to her, and I went to work, that would be about half-past-six. I finished work and got home about half-past-six in the evening. I then noticed that there were no lights in the place. I lit the gas and [it] started to go out, and I went into the bedroom to get a penny and I noticed my baby in the cot. I put the penny in the gas and went back in the bedroom. There I saw my wife lying on the bed. I spoke to her but she never answered me, so I went over and shook her, then I could see she wasn't breathing. Then I went and made some food for my baby. I fed my baby and I sat up all night.

Between about one and two in the morning I got my wife downstairs through the front door. I opened the drain outside my front door that is number 10 Rillington Place and pushed her body head first into the drain. I closed the drain then I went back in the house I sat down by the fire smoking a cigarette. I never went to work the following day. And went and got my baby looked after. Then I went and told my governor where I worked that I was leaving. He asked me the reason and I told him I had a better job elsewhere. I had my cards and money that afternoon, then I went to see a man about selling my furniture. The man came down and had a look at my furniture he offered me £40 for it. So I accepted the £40. He told me he wouldn't be able to collect the furniture until Monday morning. In the meanwhile I went and told my mother that my wife and baby had gone for a holiday. I stopped in the flat until Monday then a van came Monday afternoon and cleared the stuff out. He paid me the money. Then I caught the five-to-one train to Paddington and I came down to Merthyr Vale and I have been down here ever since. That's the lot."

In this document Evans takes responsibility for obtaining the forbidden substance but maintains that he did not wish his wife to take it. Then he has a further change of mind:

Question put by Mr Henry Elam of counsel who was examining Evans in chief: That same day did you speak to a police officer in London and again see the accused about 9 pm?

Detective Constable Howell Evans: I did. I said "The drain which you said you put your wife's body down has been examined, and there is nothing there." He replied "Well I put it there". I then asked him "is it a man-hole?" he said "I expect so." I said "Who helped you lift the lid off?" He replied "I did it myself." I said "I don't think you are physically capable of taking the lid off the man-hole. It is as much as three men can do" Evans replied "Well, I did it myself" I said "I don't think your wife's body has ever been in the drain." He then replied "No. I said that to protect a man named Christie. It is not true about the man in the café either."

There follows the second statement in which Evans, for the first time, involves John Christie:

"The only thing that is not true in the statement I made to you this afternoon is the part about meeting the man in the café and about disposing of my wife's body. All the rest is true.

As I was coming home from work one night that would be about a week before my wife died, Reg Christie who lived on the ground floor below us approached me and said 'I'd like to have a chat with you about your wife taking the tablets. I know what she is taking them for, she is trying to get rid of the baby. If you or your wife had come to me in the first place I could have done it for you without any risk'; I turned around and said 'Well I didn't think you knew anything about medical stuff' so he told me then that he was training for a doctor before the war. Then he started showing me books and things on medical. I was just as wise because I couldn't understand one word of it because I couldn't read. Then he told me that the stuff that he used, one out of every ten would die with it. I told him that I was not interested so I said goodnight to him and went upstairs.

When I got in my wife started talking to me about it. She said that she had been speaking to Mr Christie and asked me if he had spoken to me. I said yes and told her what he had spoken to me about. I turned round and told her that I told him I didn't want nothing to do with it and I told her she wasn't to have nothing to do with it either. She turned round and told me to mind my own business and that she intended to get rid of it and she trusted Mr Christie. She said he could do the job without any trouble at all.

On the Monday evening, that was the 7th November, when I came home from work my wife said that Mr Christie had made arrangements for first thing on Tuesday morning, I didn't argue with her. I just washed and changed and went to the KPH (a public house) until 10 o'clock. I came home and had supper and went to bed. She wanted to start an argument but I just took no notice of her. Just after six I got up the following morning to go to work, my wife got up with me. I had a cup of tea and a smoke and she told me "On your way down tell Mr Christie that everything is alright. If you don't tell him I'll go down and tell him myself. So as I went down the stairs he came out to meet me and said 'Everything is alright' then I went to work.

When I came home in the evening he was waiting for me at the bottom of the staircase. He said 'Go on upstairs I'll come behind you,' when I lit the gas in the kitchen he said 'It's bad news it didn't work'. I asked him where was she. He said 'Laying on the bed in the bedroom'. Then I asked him where was the baby so he said the 'baby is in the cot'; I went into the bedroom, I lit the gas, then I saw the curtains had been drawn. I looked at my wife and saw that she was covered over with the eiderdown. I pulled the eiderdown back to have a look at her, I could see that she was dead and that she had been bleeding from the mouth and nose and that she had been bleeding from the bottom part. She had a black skirt on and a check blouse and a kind of light blue jacket on. Christie was in the kitchen. I went over and picked up my baby.

I wrapped the baby in the blanket and took her to the kitchen. In the meanwhile Mr Christie had lit the fire in the kitchen. He said 'I'll speak to you after you feed the baby', so I made the baby some tea and boiled an egg for her, then I changed the baby and put her to sit in front of the fire. Then I asked him how long my wife had been dead. He said 'since about three o'clock'; then he told me that my wife's stomach was septic poisoned. He said 'another day and she'd have gone in hospital.' I asked him what he had done, but he wouldn't tell me. He then told me to stop in the kitchen, and he closed the door and went out. He came back about a quarter of an hour later and told me that he had forced the door of Mr Kitchener's flat and had put my wife's body in there. I asked him what he intended to do and he said 'I'll dispose of it down one of the drains'. He then said 'You'd better go to bed and leave the rest to me', he said 'get up and go to work in the morning' and that he'd get up and see about someone looking after my baby. I told him that it was foolish to try and dispose of the body, and he said 'well that's the only thing I can do or else I'll get into trouble with the police'. He then left me. Before I went to bed I took the eiderdown and one blanket off the bed and put them in a cupboard in the bedroom.

I got up next morning about six o'clock. I made myself a cup of tea and made the baby some breakfast fed her and changed her and put her back into her cot. Christie had told me that he was going to look after the baby that day so I went to work. I saw Christie before I went and he told me that he would slip up and feed the baby during the day. I had wanted to take the baby to my mother the night before, but he said not to as it would cause suspicion straight away. He told me in the morning that he knew a young couple over in East Acton who would look after the baby, and he'd go over and see them.

When I came home from work on that Wednesday night at about five or six Christie told me that the young couple from East Acton would be in on Thursday to take the baby.

I fed the baby that night and was playing with her by the fire when Christie came in. He said 'in the morning when you get up feed the baby and dress her then put her back in the cot, the people will be here just after 9 in the morning to fetch her'. He said 'I have told them to knock three knocks and I will let them in'. He also told me to pack some clothes for the baby. I did all that in the morning before I went to work. I saw him as I was going out that morning about half-past-six and told him what I had done.

About half past five that evening I came home. I went upstairs and as I got in the kitchen he came up behind me. He told me that the people had called and took the baby with them and to pack the rest of her things and he had a case and would take them over to Acton with the pram and her chair later in the week. I then asked him how did he dispose of my wife's body. He said he put it down one of the drains. That is all he said to me then he went downstairs. Later that evening, I went around to see my mother, Mrs Thomasina Probert, at No 11 St Mark's Road London W11. She asked me where Beryl and the baby was I told her they had gone away on a holiday. When I left my mother's place that night I went up to the KPH to have a drink.

I didn't go back to work on Friday as I had finished there on the Thursday. On that Thursday evening Christie said 'Now the best thing you can do is to sell your furniture and get out of London somewhere'. I just said 'Alright'.

On the Friday I went to see a man in Portobello Road about selling my furniture. He came down on the Friday afternoon and said it was worth £40. He told me he would pick it up on the following Monday. On the Friday I went to the pictures and the pub, and then went home to sleep. On the Saturday I did the same thing.

On Sunday afternoon I went to see a rag dealer. I met him outside a café in Ladbroke Grove, that's where he lives. I told him that if he came down to my place on the Monday there was quite a lot of rags he could have.

I got up about six o'clock on the Monday morning and ripped up all my wife's clothes and the eiderdown and cut up the blankets. The man came around just after nine o'clock and took about two sacks full and I didn't take nothing off him for them.

About three o'clock the furniture van came. They cleared all the furniture out and the bedclothes and lino, and the furniture man paid me £40 which I signed for. The only thing left in the house then was vases, a clock some dishes saucepans and a bucket, and the case with the [baby's] clothes, her pram and small chair. Christie had all that stuff. He asked me where I was going to go and I told him I didn't know. Then I got my case. I took it up to Paddington, left it in the luggage department until half-past-twelve that evening.

I went to the pictures and the pub and then I went to Paddington again and picked up my case about half-past-twelve that evening and caught the five-to-one train to Cardiff. I got to Merthyr Vale about twenty-to-seven in the morning then went to 93 Mount Pleasant and I have been there ever since."

Detective Constable Evans, further questioned, said that he saw the accused on the morning of the 1st December. He said Evans told him that he helped Christie carry the body of his wife down the stairs and into Kitchener's flat and that was the last time he saw her body. A few days later Evans called to see Christie and enquired about his child. Christie said, "She's alright, you can't see her yet, it would be too early leave her alone for about three weeks. Then write to me and I'll let you know when you can see her."

Chief Inspector George Jennings was sworn in. He told how he found the body of Beryl Evans in the wash-house, and also the body of Geraldine. He said:

> "At 9.45 pm on the 2nd December [I] saw Timothy Evans at Notting Hill Gate police station. I said 'I am Chief Inspector Jennings in charge of this case. At 11 am today I found the dead body of your wife Beryl Evans concealed in the wash-house at 10 Rillington Place, Notting Hill, also the body of your baby daughter Geraldine in the same out building and this clothing was found on them'. Later I was present at Kensington Mortuary when it was established that the cause of death was strangulation in both cases. [I said to Evans] 'I have reason to believe that you are responsible for their deaths' he said 'yes'."

Evans then made the following extraordinary statement to Jennings:

> "She was incurring one debt after another and I could not stand it anymore and took her down to the flat below the same night whilst the old man was in hospital. I waited till the Christies downstairs had gone to bed, then I took her to the wash-house after midnight. This was on Tuesday 8th November. On Thursday evening after I came home from work I strangled my baby in our bedroom with my tie and later that night I took her down into the wash-house after the Christies had gone to bed."

Evans added to his statement: "It's a great relief to get it off my chest. I feel better already. I can tell you the cause that led up to it." This short declaration was followed by the much longer confession which sealed Evan's fate:

"I was working for the Lancaster Food Products of Lancaster Road W11. My wife was always moaning about me working long hours so I left there and went to work for the Continental Wine Stores of Edgware Road. I started at 8 am and finished at 2 pm, and the job was nice there. In the meanwhile my wife got herself into £20 debt, so I borrowed £20 off the governor under false pretences, so he gave me the £20 which I took home and gave to my wife. I asked her who she owed the money to but she would not tell me, so a week later I got sacked. I was out of work then for another two or three weeks. In the meanwhile I had been driving for two or three days a week. I was earning 23 to 30 shillings a day. This was for the Lancaster Food Products. I used to give her this money and she was moaning she was not getting enough wages. So one of the regular drivers at the Lancaster Food Products left, so the governor asked me if I would like my regular job back at a wage of £5 .15 shillings a week. I was doing quite a lot of overtime for the firm, working late and I used to earn altogether £6–7 a week.

Out of that my wife used to go to the firm on a Friday and my governor used to pay her £5 what she used to sign for. Perhaps through the week I would have to give her more money off different people which I used to borrow. I used to pay them back on a Friday out of my own pocket. I had to rely on my overtime to pay my debts and then I had a letter from J Brodericks telling me I was behind in my payments for my furniture on the hire purchase, I asked her if she had been paying furniture and she said she had; then I showed her the letter I had received from Brodericks, then she admitted she hadn't been paying for it. I went down to see Broderick myself to pay them £1 a week and ten shillings off the arrears so then I left the furniture business to my wife. I then found she was in debt with the rent. I accused her of squandering the money, so that started a terrific argument in my house, I told her if she didn't pull herself together I would leave her, so she said 'You can leave any time you like' so I told her she would be surprised one day if I walked out on her. One Sunday early in September I had a terrific row with her at home so I washed and showered and went to the pub dinner time. I stopped there until two o'clock. I came home, had my lunch, left again to go out leaving my wife and baby at home because I didn't want any more arguments. I went to the pictures — ABC Lancaster

Road, known as Royalty at 4.30 pm. I came out when the film was finished I think about 7.15 pm I went home and switched the wireless on. I made a cup of tea my wife was nagging till I went to bed at 10 pm. I got up at 6 am next day, made a cup of tea. My wife got up to make a feed for the baby at 6.15 am. She gets up and starts an argument straight away. I took no notice of her and went into the bedroom to see my baby before going to work. My wife told me that she was going to pack up and go down to her father in Brighton. I asked her what she was going to do with the baby, so she said she was going to take the baby down to Brighton with her, so I said it would be a good job and load of worry off my mind so I went to work as usual so when I came home at night I put the kettle on. I sat down, my wife walked in so I said I thought you were going to Brighton? She said 'What, for you to have a good time?' I took no notice of her. I went downstairs and fetched the push chair up. I came upstairs, she started an argument again. I told her if she didn't pack it up I'd slap her face. With that she picked up a milk bottle to throw it at me. I grabbed the bottle out of her hand. I pushed her; she fell in a chair in the kitchen, so I washed and changed and went out. I went to the pub I had a few drinks I got home about 10.30 pm I walked in and she started to row again so I went straight to bed. I got up Tuesday morning and went straight to work. I came home at night about 6.30 pm my wife started to argue again, so I hit her across the face with my flat hand. The[n] she hit me with her hand. In a fit of temper I grabbed a piece of rope from a chair which I had brought home off my van and strangled her with it. I then took her into the bedroom and laid her on the bed with the rope still tied around her neck. Before 10 pm that night I carried my wife's body downstairs to the kitchen of Mr Kitchener's flat as I knew he was away in hospital. Then I came back upstairs. I then made my baby some food and fed it, then I sat with my baby by the fire for a while in the kitchen. I put the baby to bed later on. I then went back to the kitchen and smoked a cigarette. I then went downstairs when I knew everything was quiet, to Mr Kitchener's flat, I wrapped my wife's body in a blanket and a green table cloth from off my kitchen table. I then tied it up with a piece of cord from out of my kitchen cupboard. I then slipped downstairs and opened the back door, then went up and carried my wife's body down to the wash-house and placed it under the sink. I then blocked the front of the sink up with a piece of wood so that the body wouldn't be seen. I locked the wash-house door. I came in and shut the back door behind me. I then slipped back upstairs. The Christies, who live on the ground floor, were in bed. I went in the bedroom to see if my daughter was asleep. When I looked in the cot she was fast asleep so I then shut the bedroom door and laid on the bed all night until it was time to get up and go to work.

I then got up, lit the gas and put the kettle on. I made my baby a feed and fed it. I then changed her and put her back into the cot wrapping her up well so she would not get cold, then I went to the kitchen and poured myself out a cup of tea. I then finished my tea and slipped back into the bedroom to see if the baby had dropped off to sleep. It was asleep so I went off to work. I done my days work and got home about 5 pm that Wednesday evening. I came in, lit the gas, put the kettle on and lit the fire. I fed the baby had a cup of tea myself, sat in front of the fire with my baby. I made the baby a feed about 9.30 pm. I fed her then I changed her. Then I put her to bed. I came back into the kitchen, sat by the fire until about twelve o'clock, and then went to bed. I got up at 6 am next day. Lit the gas. Put the kettle on. Made the baby a feed and fed it. I then changed and dressed her. I then poured myself out a cup of tea I had already made. I drank half and the baby drank the other half. I then put the baby back into the cot, wrapped her up well and went to work. I done my days work and then had an argument with the guvnor, then I left the job. He gave me my wages before I went home. He asked me what I wanted my wages for, I told him I wanted to post some money off to my wife first thing in the morning. He asked me where my wife was and I told him she was gone to Bristol on a holiday, he said 'How do you intend to send the money to her?' I said in a registered envelope.

He paid me the money, so he said 'Call over tomorrow for your cards.' I then went home, picked up my baby from her cot in the bedroom picked up my tie and strangled her with it. I then put the baby back in the cot and sat down in the kitchen and waited for the Christie's downstairs to go to bed. At about twelve o'clock that night I took the baby downstairs to the wash-house and hid her body behind some wood. I then locked the wash-house door behind me and came in closing the back door behind me. I then slipped back upstairs and laid on the bed all night, fully clothed. I got up the following morning, washed, shaved and changed, and then went to see a man in Portobello Road about selling the furniture, I don't know his name. During the same afternoon he came to my flat, and offered me the 40 quid for it. I told him I would take the £40 for it and then he asked me why I wanted to sell it. I told him I was going to Bristol to live as I had a job there waiting for me. He asked me why I wasn't taking the furniture with me. I told him my wife had already gone there and had a flat with furniture in it. He then asked me if it was paid for. I said it was. He said he would call Sunday afternoon to let me know what time the driver would call on Monday for it. I said I would wait in for him. Between 3 and 4 on Monday this man took all the furniture, all the lino and he paid me £40 which I signed for in a receipt book.

He handed me the money which I counted in his presence. I waited till he went then picked up my suitcase which I took to Paddington. The same night I caught the 12.55 am train from Paddington to Cardiff and made my way to 93 Mount Pleasant, Merthyr Vale, where I stayed with my uncle, Mr Lynch. The rest I think you know."

Detective Inspector James Black gave evidence concerning clothing which was found at the murder scene.

Three Cases that Shook the Law

CHAPTER 23

The Defence Case

Mr Malcolm Morris then commenced his well-nigh impossible task of persuading the jury that the murder of Geraldine Evans, a defenceless baby, was committed, not by his client, an inveterate liar, but in fact by the principal witness for the prosecution, a man of commendable citizenship. His task had already been made immeasurably more difficult due to the fact that the judge had admitted statements by the defendant to the effect that in addition to the strangulation of his child he had also murdered his wife.

One wonders what the reaction of the court would have been had it been known that the worthy Mr Christie had strangled to death Ruth Fuerst and Muriel Eady; would in due course admit to the murder of Beryl Evans and would, subsequent to the trial of Timothy Evans and his execution, be convicted of the killing of Ethel Christie, Rita Nelson and Hectorina Maclennan.

Mr Morris took Evans through his statement to the police in Wales including the second in which Christie was involved as the abortionist. The reader will already be familiar with the contents from *Chapter 22*.

The point was then reached in Evans' evidence where, at Notting Hill Police Station he made the admission that he had killed his wife and child. Morris had no option but to meet it head on.

Malcolm Morris: In that statement at the beginning you speak about the way in which your wife was incurring debts did you not?
Timothy Evans: Yes.

Morris: How you had to borrow £20 from your Guv'nor and how you lost an earlier job?

Evans: Yes, sir.

Morris: Is it true that she had not paid the money you had given to her to pay hire-purchase instalments on the furniture?

Evans: Yes.

Morris: And is it true that she said she was going to pack up and go down to her father at Brighton?

Evans: Yes, sir.

Morris: Now unfortunately, as you cannot read I cannot put a statement in front of you, but perhaps you can tell my Lord and the jury this: Did you ask her if she was going with the baby, and did she say she was going to take the baby down to Brighton with her. And did you say that would be a good job and a load off your mind?

Evans: Yes. Sir.

Morris: Was all that about Monday 7th November?

Evans: Yes. Sir.

Morris: When you came home that Monday night did you say "I thought you were going to Brighton" and did she say "What for? For you to have a good time" or something like that?

Evans: That is right.

Morris: And then you say: "I took no notice of her, I went downstairs and fetched the pushchair up, I came upstairs. She started an argument again. I told her if she did not pack it up I would slap her face". Is that true?

Evans: Yes. Sir.

Morris: "With that she picked up a milk bottle and threw it at me." Is that right?

Evans: Yes, sir.

Morris: This is the Monday night, "I grabbed the bottle out of her hand. I pushed her; she fell in the chair in the kitchen, so I washed and changed and went out." That is true is it?

Evans: Yes sir, that is true

Morris: "I went to the pub and had a few drinks"?

Evans: Yes, sir.

The Defence Case

Morris: That would be the Kensington Park Hotel?

Evans: Yes.

Morris: Which you referred to as the KPH?

Evans: Yes.

Morris: "I go[t] home about 10.30 pm. I walked in. She started to row again so I went straight to bed"?

Evans: Yes, sir.

Morris: Now we come to the Tuesday morning 8th November. "I got up Tuesday morning and went straight to work."

Evans: Yes, sir.

Morris: "I came home at night about 6.30 pm?"

Evans: Yes.

Morris: Then you say my wife started to argue again so I hit her across the face with my flat hand?

Evans: Yes, sir.

Morris: Now which is true? Was she alive when you got back?

Evans: No sir. She was dead when I got home on Tuesday.

Morris: Why did you say that "In a fit of temper I grabbed a piece of rope from a chair which I had brought home off my van and strangled her with it?"

Evans: As I said before I was upset and I do not think I knew what I was saying.

Morris: Do you not think you knew what you were saying?

Evans: No sir.

Morris: Did you bring a piece of rope home from your van?

Evans: No. I had no rope in my van.

Morris: You made that up?

Evans: I made that up.

Morris: I need not go through that in detail, but later you say that on the Thursday you went home, picked up your baby from her cot in the bedroom, picked up your tie and strangled her with it. You now say that is untrue too?

Evans: That is untrue too.

Morris: And made up for the same reason?

Evans: Yes, sir.

Mr Justice Lewis: The reason being you did not know what you were saying?

Evans: Yes, sir.

Morris: Not only did you not know what you were saying, but you have given us two other reasons?

Evans: Yes sir. I was upset and I was afraid the police would take me downstairs.

Morris: Is that why you told a lie to them?

Evans: Yes, sir.

Morris: You said two things then: "I was upset and I was afraid the police would take me downstairs", when you said you were afraid the police would take you downstairs did you mean beat you up?

Evans: Yes, sir.

Morris: When you say you were upset how much were you upset?

Evans: I was pretty bad sir, I had been believing my daughter was still alive.

Morris: Had you anything left to live for when she was dead?

Evans: No, sir.

Christmas Humphreys rose to cross-examine. Never did prosecuting counsel have his work more cut out for him:

Christmas Humphreys: Is it true that on five different occasions at different places and to different persons you have confessed to the murder of your wife and child? [In fact that particular confession was made on only two occasions].

Evans: I have confessed sir, but it is not true.

Humphreys: Is it right that you have confessed it five times in different places and to different persons?

Evans: Yes it is.

Humphreys: Are you saying on each of these occasions you were upset?

Evans: The biggest part of them sir. Well, I was not upset on the five, but the last one I was.

Humphreys: If you were not upset on the five, why did you sometimes confess to wilful murder if you were not upset unless it was true?

The Defence Case

Evans: Well I knew my wife was dead; but I did not know my daughter was dead.

Humphreys: What had that got to do with it?

Evans: It had a lot to do with it.

Humphreys: Is that a reason for pleading guilty to murder, because you are upset because your daughter is dead by another person's hand?

Evans: Yes.

Humphreys: Is it?

Evans: Yes.

Humphreys: I see. Let us just look at those occasions. It is you who voluntarily go to the police on the 30th November after having read to you a letter from your mother to your aunt?

Evans: That is right.

Humphreys: It was because in the letters your previous lies were exposed that you decided to go to the police, was it?

Evans: It was not because of the lies.

Humphreys: Why did you suddenly go to the police?

Evans: Well, I was getting worried about my daughter.

Thus the cross-examination continued. Humphreys kept hammering away at the defendant about his confessions and there can be little doubt that the explanation given by Evans failed to convince the jury of even the remotest possibility of his innocence.

Three Cases that Shook the Law

CHAPTER 24

Speeches and Summing up

Christmas Humphreys made what must have been one of the shortest speeches ever for the Crown in a murder trial. He emphasised the inherent unlikelihood of Christie, a worthy citizen notwithstanding some earlier trouble, being responsible for the appalling crime with which the man in the dock stood charged. He emphasised that Christie had no possible motive for the strangulation of Geraldine. He reiterated the fact of Evans' confessions.

When Malcolm Morris rose to make the closing speech for Evans he had a mountain to climb. His was a task which in legal circles as referred to as "making bricks without — or with very little — straw." He repeated the arguments already made in examination and cross-examination and concluded with these words:

"I know his lordship will tell you that you are not to feel that he is directing you on the facts when he goes through the evidence; he directs you on the law and assists you in summing-up the facts. The facts and the witnesses as they came to give their own evidence are things for you and you alone to consider, and when you have considered them all — I ask you to say that you will look at them again and again, and in the end you will say to yourselves 'Well the case is black against him, but'— I hope I am not blinking anything in this case — 'but we are not absolutely happy, we are not absolutely certain in this case that the witness, the main witness who matters for the prosecution, Christie, was telling the truth, and if he is not, then it may be that Evans in his second statement was telling the truth, we just don't know'; and if you have looked at the facts carefully and you come to the conclusion that you just do not know, then you look into your hearts—because you will go forth after this case back to the ordinary world, and I hope you will try to forget it, of course you will if you come to the right verdict, if you are absolutely certain, but if you are not you will not forget it. So I ask you when you think about it tomorrow, to bring every effort that you conceivably can to bear, every power that you have, and when you have done that and been as careful and as fair as you can be, Evans will be satisfied and I as his advocate, cannot ask for anything more."

The opinion of a barrister as to the guilt or innocence of his or her client should the plea be one of not guilty is not relevant to his or her professional duty to present the case to the best of his or her ability. But it would seem clear from the presentation of Malcolm Morris that he did not rate the defendant's chances of an acquittal.

Mr Justice Lewis has been much criticised regarding his summing-up. It must be appreciated, however, that like everyone else involved in the trial he was totally ignorant of the true character of Christie. He explained to the jury his justification for admitting the evidence of the death of Beryl Evans, although by doing so he had brought about a greater likelihood of the conviction of Evans for the death of Geraldine. During the trial the judge frequently referred to the evidence of Christie as being that of an honest man whose account could be relied upon as against the testimony of Evans, an inveterate and admitted liar. Nowhere did he suggest that the jury should weigh the evidence of the one against that of the other. Thus, for example, he accepted without question Christie's allegation that he could not have been involved in the moving of Beryl's body because due to enteritis and fibrositis he was in no condition to pick up anything from the floor. The consequence was that the whole of Evans evidence involving Christie in claiming to be an experienced abortionist and his involvement in the death of Beryl and the subsequent disposal of her body, let alone the likelihood of his having murdered her, was completely negatived.

The judge laid great emphasis upon the plea of the prosecution that Christie had no motive for murdering the child and that in any event the cause of death was strangulation, not an attempted abortion. Little was he aware that is Christie was not, as the judge implied an abortionist, he was a strangler par excellence.

One very unattractive passage in Mr Justice Lewis's summing-up concerned the professional duty of counsel for the defence:

> "Members of the jury let me say at once; you know, counsel do not invent defences for their clients, they take their clients instructions, and do not let it be thought that I, or anybody else is suggesting that this defence was the fertile imagination of Mr Malcolm Morris. Counsel who are employed to defend people are to take the facts, what they say are the facts from the prisoner and counsel has to do the best he can with them."

Put into more colloquial language the judge is saying to the jury, "Don't be too hard on Malcolm Morris. The poor chap has to say what his client has told him to say." Mr Justice Lewis then praised the value of Christie as a believable witness. He referred to his previous convictions as being 17 years ago. Then he said:

> "Since then he has no stain on his character whatever. He is apparently happily married and is living with his wife in this ground floor flat, and is employed as a ledger clerk. It would be a terrible thing if a person who has been in trouble with the police and has had a term of imprisonment passed upon him, but has for years lived straight after that, should have it said of him that because seventeen years ago he was in trouble with the police he cannot be believed on his oath and is a practised abortionist and a murderer. That is what you are asked, in effect to say. It is entirely a matter for you and I leave it there."

The judge contrasted this with Evans' performance which from the beginning of November until the trial has been "one tissue of falsehoods from start to finish." Referring constantly to the defendant as "this man" the judge effectively demolished Evans' claim that he had been under Christie's domination or that he had any conceivably justifiable reason for killing the child.

Not surprisingly Evans was convicted of murder and sentenced to the mandatory sentence of death.

Three Cases that Shook the Law

CHAPTER 25

The Aftermath

The Lord Chief Justice delivered the judgement in the appeal. He began by stating what he regarded as the essence of the case:

"A variety of grounds have been urged by Mr Malcolm Morris on his [Evans] behalf. Objecting to evidence and various other matters in the course of the case, but there is really only one point in this case which has any substance, as with which it is necessary to deal at any length, and that is whether or not evidence with regard to statements which this man made with regard to the death of his wife and an admission on his part that he caused the death of his wife was admissible in the case.

Before the case was opened to the jury, a submission was made to Mr Justice Lewis that no evidence could be given before the jury on the case relating to the murder of the child with regard to the murder of the wife.

The learned judge overruled that submission, and he allowed the evidence which would have been given if the prisoner had also been charged with the murder of his wife, namely, these particular statements the prisoner had made. That is the evidence, in substance, which was objected to.

In the opinion of the court, the real test we have to apply here is: Was the evidence relevant, that is to say, did the statements which the prisoner made with regard to the death of his wife bear upon the question as to whether he was guilty or not guilty of the death of the child? In our opinion it is impossible to say that the evidence was not relevant; indeed it was highly relevant here where two bodies, the bodies of a mother and child, were found together in a house in which the prisoner had been living.

In our opinion the learned judge was perfectly right in admitting the evidence, and he was right in admitting the evidence because it was relevant and not on any grounds that it would be inconvenient, as it would have been, to try and disentangle the sentences which dealt with the daughter and the mother, it was one and the same story which he told. In our opinion that evidence was clearly relevant.

In these circumstances, in our opinion the prisoner was properly convicted and there is no ground for interfering with the conviction and the appeal is dismissed."

The Inquiries

The discovery that 10 Rillington Place harboured a veritable collection of dead bodies and that John Christie was a multiple murderer changed the whole situation with regard to Evans. The likelihood of two psychopathic killers in the same small house seemed an unlikely coincidence and if Evans, who had protested his innocence to all and sundry after his conviction, including to his mother and his sisters, had been wrongly convicted and executed a terrible miscarriage of justice occurred.

Under great pressure to take action the Home Secretary Sir David Maxwell Fyfe instructed the Recorder of Portsmouth, Mr John Scott Henderson QC to conduct an enquiry. The conclusion of the enquiry was that no miscarriage had taken place.

The Scott Henderson report was severely criticised on several grounds. For example, that it had been conducted with excessive and unjustified privacy, that counsel for the various parties were limited in their right to appear and participate and that the chairman had taken over the conduct of the questioning to an excessive extent.

Speeches, highly critical of the report were made in Parliament. It is not within the scope of this work to detail these, but one highly opposite contribution from Mr Geoffrey Bing is worthy of note.

The Aftermath

Mr Bing said that if Evans was guilty this depended on two incredible coincidences. The first was that in this small house in London the two male occupants were both murderers. The second was that all the murders followed the same pattern.

Ludovic Kennedy, in his book *10 Rillington Place* further points out that (the baby apart) in all cases the victims were women, murder was by strangling, sexual intercourse at the time of death took place and the bodies were similarly disposed of.

In 1965–1966 the Braden Inquiry reversed the finding of Scott Henderson. While deciding somewhat strangely that Evans had probably murdered his wife, although Christie had confessed to the crime, it was conclusive that the pardon was applicable to the murder of both his wife and child.

The alleged statement by Sir David Maxwell Fife that there is "no practicable possibility of a miscarriage of justice in a murder case in this country" is surely proved to be unsound in the light of the three cases which I have dealt with in this book.

Index

10 Rillington Place *18, 167, 234*
  description of *175*
abortion *175, 180, 185, 196, 202, 223*
accused
  testimony by *92*
admission *196*
adultery *45*
advocacy *133, 184, 188*
aiding and abetting *14, 29, 100*
alibi *18*
aliens *122, 134, 144*
allegiance *17, 122, 123, 134*
  local allegiance *137*
anti-Semitism *118*
appeal *109, 113, 123, 139, 233*
assault *171*
atmosphere *9*
Attorney-General *134, 143, 161*
autopsy *64*
Barrington, John *120*
barrister. See *counsel*
Bernstoff, Count *121*
betrayal *16*
bias *10, 105*
Bing, Geoffrey *234*
Birkbeck College *118*
Birkett, Norman *12, 184*
Black, Det Insp James *221*
Blackstone *134*

blame *189*
bodies *167, 172, 185*
Bottomly, Horatio *48*
Bow Street Magistrates' Court *122*
Braden Enquiry *235*
Brady, Ian *167*
bricks without straw *229*
Bridgeman, William *114*
Brighton *175, 181, 224*
Bristol *190, 199*
British Union of Fascists *118, 140*
broadcasting *129, 136*
broken glass *29, 64, 87, 107*
Brooklyn *118*
brutality *173*
bullying *188*
burden of proof *9, 51, 133*
Bywaters, Frederick *13, 22, 82*
'cab rank' principle *87*
callousness *173*
Carlton & Prior *22*
Casement, Roger *48, 120*
Central Criminal Court. See *Old Bailey*
Christie, Ethel *223*
Christie, John Reginald Halliday *17, 167, 189*
citizenship *133*
class *168*
Clevely, Percy Edward *76*

236

Index

common sense *9, 102*
concealment *198*
conceit *93*
confession *17, 167, 182, 185, 190, 196, 226*
conspiracy *29, 73*
  conspiracy to murder *45*
Consular Service *120*
counsel *11, 45, 87, 99, 182, 230*
courtesy *133*
Court of Criminal Appeal *109, 113, 123, 161*
credibility *18*
criminal record *171*
Crippen, Dr Hawley Harvey *48*
cross-examination *45, 92, 202, 206, 226*
Crown *87, 117, 122, 133*
  Crown prerogative *151*
culture *26*
Curtis-Bennett, Henry *12, 29, 48, 74, 92, 100, 122, 184*
daydreams *169*
death
  fascination with *170*
debts *223*
deception *37*
defence *11, 104, 105, 137, 167, 223*
demonic skill *181*
deportation *144*
depression *189*
desire *53*
Devoy, John *121*
direction *105*
divorce *87*
domicile *144*
drain *181, 191*

Drought, Dr Percy *41*
Eady, Muriel *172, 223*
East Acton *181, 192*
Easter Rising *121*
emotion *112*
Endsleigh Gardens *62, 76, 81, 108*
enticement *73*
Esher *172*
eternal triangle *13*
Europe *46*
Evans, Beryl *173, 196*
  killing of *176*
Evans, Detective Constable Howell *210, 216*
Evans, Geraldine *167, 182, 183, 184, 223*
Evans, Timothy *12, 17, 48, 167–182*
evidence *9, 45, 87, 133, 139, 233*
  admissibility *184*
  evidence of system *185*
  relevance *233*
facts
  same facts *185*
faithfulness *134*
falsehoods *180, 231*
false pretences *171*
fantasy *31, 63, 93, 169*
Fascism *118, 124*
Folkestone *140*
foreigners *145*
Foreign Office *149*
Frampton, Mr *93, 96*
Fuerst, Ruth *172, 223*
Galway *118*
gas/gassing *173, 177, 180*
Golden Age of the Bar *48*

Greenwood, Harold *47*
Grimes, Sgt Walter *79*
guile *35*
guilt *9*
gun-running *121*
Haigh, George John *48*
Hansen, William *119*
hard labour *171*
Hastings, Patrick *12, 184*
Haw-Haw, Lord. See *Joyce, William*
Hindley, Myra *167*
hire-purchase *224*
History of the Pleas of the Crown *129*
Home Secretary *114, 234*
horror *167*
House of Lords *16, 161*
Humphreys, Christmas *182, 183, 226, 229*
Humphreys, Travers *14, 47*
Hunt, Det Insp Albert *136, 140*
Ilford *13, 23, 61*
   Ilford Police Station *80*
illiteracy *169*
illusion *169*
impartiality *10, 77, 105*
incitement *51, 87, 110*
indictment *15, 51, 127, 139, 184, 195*
influence *105, 181*
innocence *9*
   protesting innocence *234*
inquisitorial system *46*
Inskip, Thomas *30, 47*
intellect *181*
IRA *118*
Ireland *17, 118*
Isle of Wight *26*

jealousy *35, 96, 111*
Jennings, Chief Inspector *193, 217*
Jews *118, 124*
Joyce, William *12, 15, 48, 117*
judges *45, 105*
   intervention by *102*
   judge made law *15*
   pitfalls *10*
jurisdiction *122, 123, 147, 149*
jury *9, 45, 105*
   direction to *47*
Kennedy, Ludovic *235*
Kensington Mortuary *193, 217*
Kensington Park Hotel *225*
knife *88, 99*
language of love *102*
last word *93*
law *133, 229*
   question of law *122*
Laxton, John *75*
letters *29, 30, 58, 63, 109, 190*
Lewis, Mr Justice *183, 198*
lies *168, 169, 189, 196, 202*
Lord Chief Justice *109, 162, 233*
loyalty *134*
Lynch, Mr and Mrs *181*
Maclennan, Hectorina *223*
magistrates' court *62*
malign feelings *63*
marriage *23*
   marital infidelity *62*
Marshall Hall, Edward *12, 49, 184*
Maxwell Fyfe, David *234*
mens rea *52*
mental issues *167, 168, 170*

Index

Merthyr Tydfil/Vale *168, 181, 191, 195, 210*
miscarriage of justice *12, 234*
Moors Murders *167*
morale *119, 124*
morality *45, 58, 102*
Morris, Malcolm *168, 184, 202, 223–227*
Mosley, Oswald *118*
motive *53, 229, 230*
  sexual satisfaction *169*
murder *45, 167, 184*
  conspiray to murder *51*
  double murder *185*
  soliciting murder *29*
mustard gas *170*
National Service *168*
National Socialist League *118*
Nazi Germany *16, 118*
Nelson, Rita *223*
New Scotland Yard *136, 140*
North Kensington *174*
Notting Hill
  Notting Hill Gate *189*
  Notting Hill Police Station *223*
Old Bailey *45, 73, 87, 170*
Oliver, Roland *47*
Paddington *178, 201, 216*
pardon
  posthumous pardon *18, 168*
  Royal pardon *235*
partiality *61*
passion *30, 45, 63, 102, 110*
passport *123, 131, 135*
persuasion *133*
Pittard, Dora *76*
poison *29, 51, 64, 87, 107*

police *170, 178*
  War Reserve Police *171*
post mortem *41*
potion *196*
prejudice *18, 62, 71, 186*
probation *171*
propaganda *127, 129*
prosecution *87, 189*
  prosecution-minded *10*
prostitution *172*
protection *134*
psychopathy *171, 234*
pubic hair *180*
public gallery *45*
Putney *173*
rag-and-bone man *192*
reciprocity *134, 141*
Reid, Lord *52*
residence *146*
respectability *170, 202*
retribution *117*
romanticism *13, 26*
Russell, Charles *184*
Russia *125*
Scott Henderson, John *234*
Seddon, Frederick *48*
seduction *24*
self-centredness *93*
self-defence *87, 99*
Sellars, Detective Inspector *80*
sentence *46*
separation *87, 93, 176*
serial killer *167, 169, 196*
Shawcross, Hartley *133, 135, 143*

Shearman, Mr Justice 42, 46, 73, 100, 105, 113
Slade, G 136, 137, 138, 143, 145, 146–150, 153–154, 159, 161
Smith, George Joseph 48
soliciting 51
South Wales 168
Special Branch 136, 140
special constable 171
Spilsbury, Bernard 64, 86, 102
stabbing 41, 88
statements 80, 210
   conflicting statements 187
Stephen, Mr Justice 52
stigma of divorce 31
strangulation 167, 177, 182, 185, 193, 196, 217
suicide 177, 179, 198
summing-up 10, 39, 42, 105–112, 229
system 185
Teare, Dr Robert 193, 196
tea room 71
temper 219, 225
theatre 24
theft 171
Third Reich 117
Thompson, Edith 12, 21–33
Thompson, Percy 13, 22–33
Thorley, Beryl 168
treachery 16
treason 15, 48, 117, 133
   high treason 128
   Treason Act 1351 122, 127, 149
   Treason Act 1945 121
Treasury Counsel 184

trust 26, 176
Tucker, Mr Justice 123, 138, 161
veracity 79
verdict 47
   erroneous verdict 11
   unsafe verdict 12
victims 172, 235
violence 24, 28, 118, 171, 225
Von Bulow, Prince 121
Waddington, Ethel 170
Waddington, Henry 172
Wales 189
war 124
   First World War 120, 170
   Second World War 117, 184
   War Reserve Police 171
Watson, Bertrand 122
Webber, John 42, 77
Webster, Mr 102
Wensley, Detective Inspector 44, 79
West, Rebecca 129
Whiteley, Cecil 48, 87, 99
White, Margaret Cairns 119
Wilde, Oscar 48
wisdom 11
witnesses 44, 45, 168, 229
women
   outlook towards 170
Young, Filson 111

Murderers or Martyrs
George Skelly
Foreword by Lord Goldsmith

A spell-binding account of an appalling miscarriage of justice. Charged with the "Cranborne Road murder" of Wavertree widow Alice Rimmer, two Manchester youths were hastily condemned by a Liverpool jury on the police-orchestrated lies of a criminal and two malleable young prostitutes. George Skelly's detailed account of the warped trial, predictable appeal result courtesy of 'hanging judge' Lord Goddard and the whitewash secret inquiry will enrage all who believe in justice. And if the men's prison letters (including from the condemned cells) sometimes make you laugh, they will make you weep far longer.

'A very powerful case of a miscarriage of justice':
Former Attorney General Lord Goldsmith PC QC

Paperback & ebook | ISBN 978-1-904380-80-1 | 2012 | 480 pages + 8 pages of photos

www.WatersidePress.co.uk

**The Cameo Conspiracy:
A Shocking True Story of Murder and Injustice**
George Skelly
THIRD EDITION

The true story of Liverpool's Cameo Cinema murders vividly demonstrates the need to guard against police corruption and legal manipulation. George Kelly was hanged in 1950 for shooting dead two men early in 1949: the manager of the Cameo Cinema, Wavertree and his assistant. Undeniably from the wrong side of the tracks and involved in petty crimes of the post-Second World War era, Kelly and his co-accused Charles Connolly (who went to prison for ten years) found themselves expertly 'fitted-up' as riff-raff in a Kafkaesque nightmare. A superbly worked account of an astonishing miscarriage of justice.

'One man's hunt for the truth':
Liverpool Echo

Paperback & ebook | ISBN 978-1-904380-72-6 | 2011 | 368 pages | 3rd edition

www.WatersidePress.co.uk

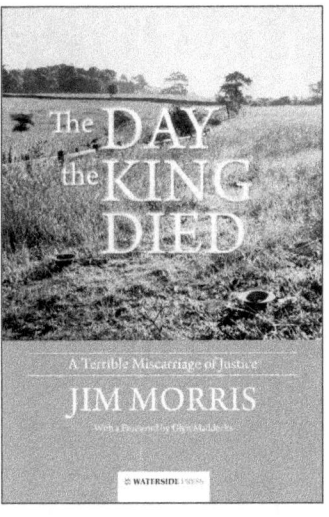

The Day the King Died:
A Terrible Miscarriage of Justice
Jim Morris
Foreword by Glyn Maddocks

There was a quaint British convention under which executions were stopped and sentence commuted if scheduled to take place on the day the sovereign died. Alfred Moore was doubly unfortunate: still protesting his innocence he was on the scaffold an hour before the death of King George VI was announced. Here, the author re-assesses the evidence in this case of the double murder of two police officers and shows why the trial at Leeds Assizes was a travesty of justice.

'A further example of why judicial homicide should never return … a readable and highly detailed account … should be compulsory reading for all law students and criminologists who become associated with our modern criminal justice processes':
Phillip Taylor MBE and Elizabeth Taylor, Richmond Green Chambers

Paperback & ebook | ISBN 978-1-909976-13-9 | 2015 | 240 pages

www.WatersidePress.co.uk

www.ingramcontent.com/pod-product-compliance
Lightning Source LLC
Chambersburg PA
CBHW070801230426
43665CB00017B/2444